# ELK COUNTRY

Text by
**Valerius Geist**

Photography by
**Michael H. Francis**

## NorthWord
PRESS, INC

BOX 1360, MINOCQUA, WI 54548

Designed by Origins Design, Inc.
Typesetting by Cavanaugh Ink.

NorthWord Press, Inc.
Box 1360
Minocqua, WI 54548

For a Free Catalog describing NorthWord's line of nature books and gifts,
call 1-800-336-5666.

ISBN 1-55971-128-0

Printed in Singapore through Palace Press, San Francisco

For me, there is no North American mammal that so wholly represents the notion of wilderness—unfettered things and untrammeled places—as does the elk. And I'm not quite sure why.

There is the bison, but it is more symbolic of a bygone era, and certainly now is in fewer numbers and occupies a relatively restricted range…a curiosity and magnificent anachronism. There is the grizzly, but it trips in my mind mostly a feeling of awe and trepidation and, when I'm in its haunts, in my very soul and marrow. There is the caribou, a truly wondrous animal, but a bit too predictable …it's there or it's not. There is the wolf, whose much-maligned and falsely impugned nature has made it seem more mythical than real. There are, too, the pronghorn, wolverine, musk-ox, bighorn sheep, mountain lion, river otter, polar bear, whitetail, Arctic fox and others that can conjure images and an atavistic chord of a more pristine time and sensible natural order. For me, only the clever coyote comes close to the elk as representative of wild America. And, again, I'm not quite sure why.

Perhaps I feel that way because, like the coyote, the elk survived and now thrives quite well despite the incursions, inventions, insensitivities and tenacity of the human animal. Perhaps it's because, in an eyeblink of evolutionary time, the species (though not all its subspecies) adapted to habitats that humans have yet to overwhelm with shopping malls, fast-food stores, landfills and hurdy-gurdy traffic.

There is the elk's size, pelage, antlers and its more-than-eerie tremulous bugle. It is a remarkable animal—to locate, observe, study, hunt, photograph, but mostly just to know … that it exists and persists in many of the continent's primitive strongholds.

Like no other animal, the elk has challenged my academic ken and, in its pursuit afield, all my sensory faculties.

I am a student of wildlife, and the mysteries of the elk have not been answered easily or at all. The more I have discovered about the species, and the more frequently I have witnessed elk, the more there is to explore … and *want* to learn.

Among various anthropomorphic terms used to describe elk, "regal" and "majestic" seem to be used most of all. It may be both of these … but for me, the elk is more so a ghost—not an apparition, but a very real animal that somehow provides a temporal and visceral link between the ecological purity and integrity of North America's past and the remnants of such today.

I "met" Valerius Geist in 1977. I knew of his work before then, and doubt that he knew of mine. We were brought together by the vagaries of wildlife science—he as contributing author to a book for which I was the technical editor. Val had authored a chapter on big game behavior— a complicated synthesis, to be sure.

I very well recall reading Val's manuscript at least three times even before taking a firm grip on my obdurates red pen. The style was a strange blend of hard European science and New World popular prose. The entire manuscript was fashioned as a panoply of hypotheses ... a rather ingenious approach. But even more unique than Val's writing style was how succinctly and often simply he constructed or characterized animal behavior. It all made sense ... in fact, too much sense sometimes. What Val described or explained in many cases far exceeded my prior understanding or willingness to accept.

Among the points of dilemma, for example, was Val's contention that the timing of birthing of certain large ungulates—such as the caribou and Africa's gnu—was an "adaptive antipredator strategy" to "swamp" the calving range, and thereby increase the likelihood of individual calf survival. Good grief, I thought (and actually wrote in the margin), that implies a significant and serious level of cognition on the part of animals that aren't known for premeditation.

In all, there were no less than 20 such points. Normally, I send an author a detailed list of questions for clarification or reconsideration. With Val's manuscript, I felt I was on particularly "soft ground." If I successfully challenged or modified one behavioral construction, might it not topple others that logically followed—a potentially confusing and awkward domino effect?

On the other hand, to accept unquestioningly Val's characterizations of certain behaviors was, in effect, validating perhaps forever those explanations, however well-reasoned and/or logical. And in wildlife science, nothing is as dynamic and fraught with exceptions as is animal behavior ... depending as it does on time, place and circumstance. For that reason, when someone as learned as Val Geist defines a

behavior in the professional literature, it tends to become fact ... regardless of time, place or circumstance. I hoped then (and know now) that Val's interpretations were just that—interpretations—and that he did not intend them as summary, but rather as "new and improved" vantage points of and for better understanding of individual animals, populations and species.

Faced with that dichotomy, I did what very few stymied technical editors would do—first, I admitted to an impasse; second, I telephoned Val. It was the start of a very constructive and rewarding push-me-pull-you relationship. And it has continued since, by phone and correspondence, and for several other books on big game species on which we collaborated. I learned that Val's hypotheses are based on careful research and incredibly thoughtful insight into the very processes of evolution and survival, not only of the species in question, but of animals worldwide from the same taxonomic order and family, including their phylogenetic ancestors. I learned, too, that Val speaks and writes confidently, often categorically, from the "bottom line" ... but a bottom line that has been painstakingly analyzed. So one doesn't just absorb from him; one has to reckon with him as well. For his part, I'm sure, Val learned patience with technical editors.

(Incidentally, the concept of "swamping" is alive and well. If it has validity, it was "programmed" in certain cervids through the ages and is not a consequence of reasoning.)

I greatly respect what Val Geist communicates about wildlife, particularly North American big game. He, too, is a student of their habitats and ways … and an especially good student. Furthermore, Val is a first-rate biologist, scholar and teacher. Those in his audience cannot miss or mistake the conviction and passion in his words, and they are well-advised not to ignore them.

So much did I come to respect Val's experiences and perceptions that, when working on other books to which he was not a contributor, I sought and invariably used his opinions and wisdom on befuddling questions about wildlife behavior and interrelationships.

We still disagree … sometimes. In this work, for example, Val paints a somewhat cloudy picture about the future of elk. I am considerably less pessimistic. But make no mistake, the fringes of gloom that Val addresses are quite real prospects that can impinge on our natural heritage, including wildlife … and I heed his warnings. To be certain, Val observes that elk and other wildlife are endangered in figurative and literal contexts by a human society unwittingly or myopically accepting a second-rate environment. His message is not one of doom, but one of caution. And I don't disagree with that.

We need elk … as we need grasses, mountains, coyotes and clear sky … because they are part of *our* nature, *our* wilderness … because they are regal and majestic … because they are our ghosts …

**Richard E. McCabe**
*Secretary, Wildlife Management Institute*

Alberta, Canada, when the grizzly appeared and charged. Although I normally roam the woods alone, I'm glad that on this trip Conrad was by my side. At six feet we stopped the charging bear with Counter Assault, a red pepper-based repellent similar to Mace.

So, I'd like to say a special thanks to my friend Conrad Rowe because we shared one elk trip that neither one of us will ever forget. By the way, the bull elk we were following watched the whole episode and never moved.

Many other people along the way helped me with this book.

As always, without the support of my wife, Victoria, there wouldn't be a book. She and my daughters, Elizabeth and Charlotte, spent long periods of time alone, yet the needed encouragement to keep me focussed on my goals was always there.

**S**it back for a moment and think about what you would do if you were in this situation: A sow grizzly bear with cubs is charging. You have only a matter of seconds to react. Do you run, climb a tree, play dead or maybe use a weapon or repellent spray?

While photographing elk, fellow photographer Conrad Rowe and I had to make that decision. We were following a nice bull elk in the wilds of

Special thanks to Ron Shade, a nature cinematographer whose wanderings often bring him into good wildlife country. Thanks for so often sharing those secret spots.

To Jim and Mary McCaleb, thanks for always making me feel welcome in your home.

I especially with to thank Dr. Valerius Geist. Without his informative text this wouldn't be much of a book. I hope between his writing and drawings and my photography we can bring you, the reader, with us into the wilds of elk country.

*Michael Francis*

Valerius Geist is a professor of environmental sciences on the Faculty of Environmental Design at the University of Calgary at Alberta, Canada. He obtained a Ph.D. in zoology in 1966, specializing in ethology (the study of animal behavior), from the University of British Columbia, Vancouver, where he worked with Dr. Ian McTaggert-Cowan, whose work on the taxonomy of mule deer (1936) remains definitive to this day.

After a year of post-doctoral study in Germany with Konrad Lorenz, Dr. Geist took a position at the University of Calgary where he became a founding member of the Faculty of Environmental Design as its first Program Director for Environmental Sciences. He published one technical (1971) and one popular book (1975) on his work with mountain sheep and edited, with Fritz Walther in 1974, a two-volume conference proceedings on the behavior of ungulates. He has also been a consultant or co-editor for numerous other books, including some published by the National Geographic Society. Currently he is completing a monograph on the deer family.

His scientific work has been honored by the American Association for the Advancement of Science, The Wildlife Society, the Foundation for North American Wild Sheep and other organizations.

In addition to his published technical works, Geist has had more than 70 popular articles published in outdoor and natural history magazines. He is the wildlife columnist for *Western Sportsman* magazine and serves on the editorial boards of numerous scholarly journals.

Dr. Geist's research has focused mainly on the biology and evolution of large Ice Age mammals, but also on policy matters in wildlife conservation. The basis of his research for this book stems from field and experimental studies of mule and white-tailed deer that were done primarily since 1969.

Conservation is a major focus of Val Geist's work. He acts as an expert witness in investigations pertaining to breaches of conservation legislation in Canada and the United States, in environmental impact assessments and public hearings. He serves on committees with the International Union for the Conservation of Nature, the Conseil International de la Chasse, Wildlife Habitat Canada, The World Wildlife Fund, Canadian Society of Zoologists, Alberta Society of Professional Biologists, The Canadian Committee for the International Biological Programme, the Frankfort Zoological Society and others.

Val met his wife, Renate, when both studied biology at the University of British Columbia. She teaches German and is a translator with several published volumes to her credit. The Geists have three grown children, a daughter and two sons, and are now grandparents. Renate is an avid gardener and hiker, Val a wilderness buff, hunter and fisherman.

# ELK ◗ COUNTRY

To Greg & Nina,
Welcome to Montana
and watch out for the
bears.
                Best regards from
                The photographer.
                    Michael H. Francis
                        1992

# PROLOGUE

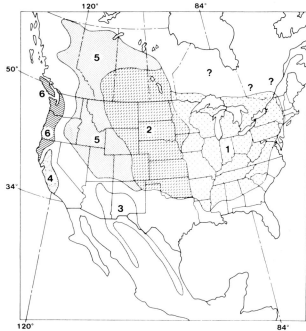

*Original distribution of 1. Eastern elk, 2. Manitoban elk,
3. Merriam Elk, 4. Tule elk, 5. Rocky Mountain elk, and 6.
Roosevelt elk, based on available records.
— Courtesy of the Wildlife Management Institute*

Late on August 17, 1886, Captain Moses Harris rode at the head of M Troop, 1st U.S. Cavalry, into Mammoth Hot Spring, Yellowstone National Park. There he was to relieve the capable but unfortunate park superintendent of his duties. Yellowstone was under siege, in need of army protection. In 1886 commercial poaching in the park by "hiders," and "tuskers" killing elk for their upper canine teeth, was rampant. Tourists were destroying national geologic treasures, wielding axes and hammers to smash souvenirs from pristine mineral surface deposits. Free-roaming cattle were despoiling the vicinity of hot springs, and forest fires, set deliberately or carelessly by campers, were scorching the back country.

Captain Harris gained jurisdiction of Yellowstone from a discredited civil administration led by a succession of powerless superintendents — some good, capable but frustrated men, others scoundrels bent on defrauding the public for personal gain, and all abandoned by an uncaring Congress in the distant East.

Lobbies were already afoot to privatize and dissect the park and build tourist attractions. The plunder of the continent was under way, in particular of its wildlife resources. In 1886 the days of the buffalo were over, but Captain Harris didn't know that. Nobody did. For several years, however, hide hunters would still organize parties to search for buffalo that they thought must be somewhere. It took time for the hunters and others to realize that the buffalo bonanza was over. Elk, bighorn sheep, and deer were next in line for decimation and were already bearing heavy losses to commercial hunting.

It is ironic that the U.S. Army was to come to the rescue of Yellowstone's wildlife, for the demise of these animals had actually been planned, in part, by the U.S. Army.

After the U.S. Civil War, pioneer growth toward the Pacific, and thus to the "manifest destiny" of America, was encountering resistance from troublesome bands of Indian warriors. Determined to keep whites out of Indian lands, these warriors proved almost undefeatable in battle. Clever men, highly skilled in guerilla warfare, and fighting in a land they knew intimately well, they made mockery of U.S. Army efforts to contain them. The Indians were highly mobile and needed no supply lines. They took what they needed from the land.

The Indians were feared, and with good reason. George Armstrong Custer's humiliating performance in the 1867 campaign against the Sioux and Cheyennes in Kansas made it clear that the Indian "problem" could not be resolved by conventional military means. Their small numbers notwithstanding, as long as the Indians could live off the land, they would make shambles of any plan to curtail their freedom. Generals William T. Sherman and Philip H. Sheridan, protagonists of total war with the Indians, saw that clearly. To bring the tribes to their knees, they devised a new strategy: destroy the Indian base of operations — destroy wildlife. The strategy worked only too well.

*A successful hunt in Yellowstone Park, 1871.*
*The Hayden Expedition.*
*– Photo courtesy of the National Park Service.*

**PROLOGUE**     19

In fairness, though, the U.S. Army only abetted what had already begun. An insatiable luxury market for wildlife in major American cities was now linked via rail lines to an apparently endless supply of wildlife on the frontier. The army aided the transfer of wildlife to the East by protecting the railways and making the bloody work of market hunters as safe and effective as possible. This sanguinary plunder was not restricted to whites. Some native people joined commercial hunters in the profitable destruction of western wildlife while it lasted.

And wildlife, especially buffalo, didn't last long. Even in Canada, in the absence of the U.S. Army's decimation policy, buffalo were disappearing so quickly that, by 1857, Cree Indians were opposing western intrusions by the mixed-blood metis from the province of Manitoba to the east. By 1873 the southern North America bison herd was exterminated, and in 1883 the last great slaughter, in Montana, terminated the northern herd. Now the destruction was to shift to other species, especially elk.

I n 1875 a disgusted General William E. Strong, witnessing the thousands of skeletons bleaching around Mammoth Hot Spring, condemned the slaughter of elk in Yellowstone, which was signed into being as a national park by President Ulysses S. Grant on March 31, 1872. Other officers shared Strong's sentiment. Elk were being killed commercially for hides, tongues and "tusks," but along with a dwindling number of buffalo, continued to exist in the park. General Sheridan, who in 1875 was espousing before the Texas legislature the need to eliminate the last bison in Texas, was having

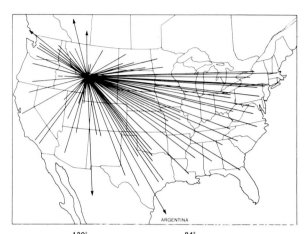

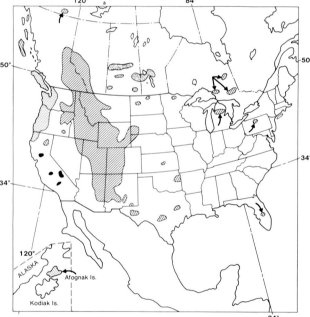

☒ Manitoban; ■ Tule; ☒ Roosevelt; ☒ Rocky Mountain;
☒ Rocky Mountain Transplants

*(Top) Destinations of live elk shipments from Yellowstone Park, 1892-1967. Courtesy of the Wildlife Management Institute.*
*(Bottom) Distribution of elk in North America as of 1978, based on the compilation of information provided by provincial and state wildlife agencies.*
*– Courtesy of the Wildlife Management Institute.*

second thoughts by 1880. He condemned the market hunters and was to become a convert to conservation. Although an act of 1884 extended Wyoming law to Yellowstone National Park, granting some protection to wildlife, it was ineffective in halting the carnage. So in 1886, Sheridan sent in the army.

It was under Sheridan's orders that Captain Harris and M Troop entered Yellowstone on August 17 of that year, the first day of modern wildlife management in North America. Harris immediately began to assert army control over the park. This control would continue for 32 years and would save from destruction an American idea that would be emulated worldwide, the idea of national parks. Captain Harris' arrival was the beginning of a legacy of U.S. and Canadian armed forces conserving wildlife on military land. And despite great difficulties, Harris and his U.S. Cavalry followers would save from extinction the last vestiges of free-living plains bison and, very likely, the elk as well.

Providence played a hand in choosing the first three U.S. Army captains who served as protectors of Yellowstone. They were brave and competent men undaunted by their task. Above all, they were endowed with vision and a will to act. They were the strict, clever Moses Harris, the indomitable F.A. Boutell, and the visionary George S. Anderson. They were all resourceful men, too.

They had to be because they had little legislated power of authority. Congress would not grant such until the passage of the Yellowstone Park Protection Act of 1894, when the public, disturbed by the loss of wildlife in the park,

prodded lawmakers into action. Until then the soldiers had to rely on force of personality, audacity, and craftiness to get their way.

Before the 1894 legislation, all the soldiers could do was turn a poacher out of the park. Initially, the army confiscated poachers' equipment, until a court declared this action was illegal. There were no laws, however, that specified where and when a culprit was to be turned loose. Caught in the south of the park, a poacher might be marched on foot across Yellowstone for release at the northern boundary. He would then be informed to collect his gear at the opposite corner of the park. Some poachers were put in a guardhouse while a request was telegraphed to Washington for instructions on what to do about them. Such requests were sure to take time to reach the capital, and there to receive lengthy bureaucratic consideration before replies were tendered. Some poachers received a hearty thrashing, effective in every case.

The cavalry troops went on park border patrols, snowshoed into distant corners of the park in winter, and made their presence known to locals who had little but contempt for restrictions on their freedom to roam about and do as they pleased. The soldiers also supervised tourist traffic and did their best to end vandalism of natural sites. Praised for being courteous but firm, these soldiers were models for the park wardens that were to follow them, but not for another thirty years.

While protecting park wildlife, the cavalry officers made friends and allies, including visiting Congressmen and the capable George Bird Grinnell, editor of *Forest and Stream* magazine. The officers also got to know their antagonists, both local and distant. Captain

Harris, for instance, not only prohibited the killing of park game, he also banned the sale of fish caught in the park and denied the commercial import of any game killed outside the park for consumption within it boundaries. The tourist industry in the park howled at this, but Harris had support from General Sheridan and from Washington. Thirty years later, Harris' protection stratagem was recognized as the most important policy of wildlife protection, a cornerstone of North American wildlife management. The benefit of prohibiting markets in dead wildlife thus had a well-tested history long before it was declared law in the U.S. in 1915 and in Canada by 1921.

Beyond the tiny remnants of countryside where North American wildlife was being protected

by the U.S. Army, however, the slaughter continued and was not to abate for another forty years, a decade longer in Canada. Railroad and mining crews were still sustained on wild game. Farmers were driving pigs into pelican colonies and the nesting grounds of pigeons. Punt gunners maintained a steady supply of waterfowl to jaded palates in large eastern cities. Buffalo hunters were turning their attentions to other game.

As wildlife populations collapsed under the onslaught, public sentiment was roused towards protection. In 1902 Theodore Roosevelt addressed Congress on the need specifically to protect elk. Elk population declines prompted the Benevolent and Protective Order of the Elks to request from

*Large herds of wintering elk are evidence of the success in restoring this species in North America. Many foreign countries envy us this achievement.*

PROLOGUE          23

Congress a ten-year moratorium on elk hunting. The Teton Game Reserve of 1905 gave elk more needed protection. In 1907 President Roosevelt and the Wyoming State Legislature asked the Elks to abandon carrying elk tusk ornaments to remove a lucrative market from poachers. The Grand Elks Lodge, prompted by Wyoming State Game Warden D.C. Nowlin in 1908, took the initial steps in establishing a national elk refuge. A study commissioned by the lodge expounded the need for habitat as crucial to elk conservation, and, in 1912, the National Elk Refuge became a reality. By then, however, elk were extirpated from almost ninety percent of their former range.

Between 1906 and 1921, foundations were laid for the recovery of North America's wildlife.

The Boone and Crockett Club was then very instrumental in fostering sound policies for wildlife conservation. President Theodore Roosevelt and Canadian Prime Minister Sir Winfred Lourier, close friends and pioneer conservationists, made sure that we have today a system of North American management and conservation of wildlife. William T. Hornaday and C. Gordon Hewitt vigorously publicized the plight of America's wildlife and were instrumental in drafting model legislation that eventually passed in all states and provinces. Gifford Pinchot and Sir Clifford Sifton, respectively, ably guided the debate about wildlife's future in the Commissions on Conservation in the U.S. and Canada. These leaders and others plowed the ground that Aldo

Leopold and others would sow, and which later would blossom and prosper. A new era was dawning. The return, or at least partial return, of wildlife had begun. The tragic lessons of unbridled exploitation, and the consequent fate that had befallen our wildlife, had been learned.

The conservation efforts of the U.S. Cavalry would come to fruition in the early 1900s when Yellowstone National Park became the center from which elk were distributed for reintroduction continent-wide. Elk went south for transplant as far as Mexico, north to Alberta, east to New York, west to Washington, into virtually every state in the Union. Hundreds of Yellowstone elk were imported between 1917 and 1920 into Alberta alone to start new herds or to add to the stragglers from British Columbia that survived the great demise.

*The alpine meadow, rich in flowers and forbs, is the natural nursery of elk calves in the West.*

Vigorous elk reintroduction programs continued to flourish for over half a century. Herds grew in states and provinces across the continent, making elk once again a fairly common, highly valued game animal. With the success, this renewed abundance and return to game animal status, the elk's chances for long-term survival were greatly enhanced. Conservation-minded hunters and others who had already fought so diligently for elk preservation would now speak even more eloquently and forcefully in the animal's behalf.

The strongest voice for the elk has been the Missoula, Montana based Rocky Mountain Elk Foundation. Since its inception in 1984, the Foundation has worked diligently to preserve

elk habitat. The Foundation, backed by 75,000 members, spearheaded the effort to protect critical elk wintering range north of Yellowstone National Park. Their quarterly publication, The Bugle, provides a forum for dialogue on conservation issues related to elk management.

So, today when you see herds of wintering elk, when you hear the bugling of bulls reverberate in mountain valleys, and thrill to the sight of elk calves gamboling in green summer meadows, remember the animals elk are alive today not because of the grace of nature. They are alive because of a man-made rescue of America's wildlife. Remember, too, those people who stood guard and rescued our elk and other wildlife. Remember those who cared for North America's wildlife in its blackest hour.

# FROM BEYOND SIBERIA

The elk of North America belong to the red deer species, *Cervus elaphus,* named in Latin in 1758 by Swedish biologist Carl von Linne. He is better known to us in the Latin form, Carolus Linnaeus.

Linnaeus named the red deer from animals he knew from southern Sweden. They were deer related to, but distinct from, North American elk. Scientists recognize such distinctions within a species by naming subspecies. The red deer known to Linnaeus is the West-European red deer, *Cervus elaphus elaphus* (Linnaeus, 1758).

The red deer is a species with many diverse subspecies. Its giants once matched Alaska bull moose in size, its dwarfs were no larger than Florida key deer. Both extremes are now extinct. However, the living red deer are spectacular enough. They range from populations dwarfed by poor habitat in dense "industrial" conifer forests in Austria to long-eared, gray, mule-deer-like highland deer in Tibet and Ganzu Province of China; to small forest wapiti with notoriously small antlers in Manchuria and eastern China; to small island deer in Sardinia; to peculiar Ice Age relics in southern Spain; to big, tall-antlered open-country forms that are dispersed throughout North America, but in Siberia and Mongolia are confined to the highlands.

Our North American elk has many synonyms. It was first named a subspecies, *Cervus elaphus canadensis,* by Erxleben in 1777; it was elevated subsequently to a full species in 1780 by Borowski. Granting individual species status to particular animal forms was common in those early days of classification. Taxonomists at that

*Thermal areas, such as those in Yellowstone National Park, can be highly coveted habitat for elk. Elk not only feed on green grasses growing along the warm streams in winter, they may use the streams to take warm baths.*

**FIGURE 1.**
(Top) This drawing depicts the size differences in wapiti, comparing the small Alashan wapiti in the foreground with the Rocky Mountain elk in the middle and the shaded giant, the extinct "cave stag" which was as large as an Alaska bull moose. All three are depicted in the herding posture of harem-holding bulls.

**FIGURE 2.**
(Bottom) Depicted here are the differences in mouth shaping by Rocky Mountain wapiti and West European red deer during bugling and roaring, respectively. The red deer forms a large resonating chamber with its mouth, minimizing the mouth opening to produce the low-frequency roars that are reminiscent of a tiger's territorial call. The low-frequency roar carries well in dense vegetation. The elk's high-pitched bugle is structured to carry long distances.

time classified "species" according to external differences. Today, however, we recognize as a species a group of regional populations that potentially form an interbreeding whole. By this definition, our elk is a subspecies of red deer, even though it is quite different from the red deer of Europe and central Asia. Different though the elk may be from the distant red deer of Europe, it is progressively less different from red deer as we move from west to east across the vast expanse of Eurasia. In the northeastern part of Asia, red deer are elk-like, and in Mongolia even identical to the North American elk.

We now recognize the elk as a subspecies of red deer and label it *Cervus elaphus canadensis* (Erxleben, 1777). At this point controversy sets in, though, for currently up to six subspecies are recognized in North America, a state of affairs not likely to prevail if taxonomists realize how much environment affects differences between populations. These regional "subspecies" are *canadensis* (Erxleben, 1777), the Eastern elk, now long extinct but once quite abundant in Ontario, southern Quebec, Pennsylvania, New York, Virginia, Georgia, Alabama and Louisiana. These states and provinces hardly strike us as "elk states" today, yet remarkable numbers of elk once lived in these areas, in some cases as little as 150 years ago. (President Teddy Roosevelt recorded in his account of elk that the last of the Alleghenies elk was killed in Pennsylvania in 1869.) All that is left for us of this once abundant deer—a few incomplete skulls and one faded skin—resides in museums.

On the opposite side of the continent one finds the Roosevelt elk, *roosevelti* (Merriam, 1897). It was named in the days when zoologists labeled formally anything they felt was different, without being aware that some of the differences are not genetic in origin but are normal growth responses of animals to differences in amount and patterning of nutrients during the annual cycle. The Roosevelt elk of the Pacific Coast in northern California, Oregon, Washington and Vancouver Island is usually a large-bodied elk. However, it grows antlers that show some growth deficiencies and are thus often different from those of other elk. Thus, the Roosevelt elk is an *ecotype*, reflecting, in size and structure, dominant aspects of west coast ecology. One such ecological aspect is the rather poisonous, fast-growing and quickly fibrous but abundant vegetation, such as the dense salal thickets, typical of that region.

A vivid account is given of the home of the Roosevelt elk by T. S. van Dyke in a book on American deer co-authored in 1901 with America's great hunter and naturalist President, Theodore Roosevelt. Van Dyke dwells on what a hunter determined to follow elk is likely to encounter in the virgin forests of redwood, douglas firs and cedars. He describes the fallen trunks draped with moss, the tall ferns, salal thickets, salmonberries and vine maple, of the deep gorges filled with rushing streams, the steep-sloped, rainy headwaters of streams where elk often dwell, and on the difficulties of closing with the elusive quarry and seeing it in the tangle.

There is little to suggest that the Roosevelt elk is a true subspecies. If it were a true subspecies, there should be something unique to all individuals of these west coast elk, some characteristic by which one can identify such elk, regardless of where they are. While this can be done with, for instance, the Manchurian wapiti from Siberia, it cannot be done with North American wapiti. When looking at captive American elk, there is no way to tell their geographic origin. This is true even for the smallest of our wild elk, the dwarf or Tule elk of California, *nannodes* (Merriam, 1905). They grow into large-bodied elk if given adequate nutrition in captivity, and nothing then betrays their geographic origins. Yet, captive or not, a Manchurian wapiti could be recognized as such at a glance by someone with the required expertise. Consequently, early taxonomists often labeled ecotypes as subspecies, a state of affairs that has, I regret to say, persisted in North America.

The Tule elk, or California elk, is named after the dense tule marshes that once fringed the streams and lagoons leading into San Francisco Bay. The name "Tule," however, may be a misnomer. In early times this elk roamed in huge herds, together with countless pronghorns, the expansive, dry, coverless San Joaquin Valley. However, it sought refuge in the tule swamps once the demand for meat by gold miners made it a prime target of market hunters. Van Dyke well describes the tule environment: "The tule is a spongy, round reed, some fifteen feet long, growing from shallow water, and so dense that half a dozen stalks to the square foot, an inch to an inch and a half in diameter, are common. Back of this, on the dryer ground, are cattails and flag, very rank and tall, so that the whole is about equal to the heaviest canebreak, though not quite as stiff in the individual stalks."

Before searching refuge in these thickets, California elk lived like some African plains antelope. They roamed in huge herds the San Joaquin Valley's coverless plains. Nor were these California elk dwarfs, as the alternative common name "dwarf elk" suggests. They were, according to van Dyke, a trifle smaller than Rocky Mountain elk, but he noted that the difference was not great.

Other geographic variants of North American elk named as subspecies are the Rocky Mountain elk, *nelsoni* (Bailey, 1935), which ranges from New Mexico north to north-central British Columbia (and has been introduced from Yellowstone National Park to many localities on this continent and beyond).

Like other "subspecies" that range north and south, northern Rocky Mountain elk are larger than the southern ones, but there are exceptions. Far to the south, in the mountains of Arizona, there once lived a large elk, the Merriam elk, *merriami* (Nelson, 1902). The Merriam elk ranged into northern Mexico, about as far south as North American elk ever spread. The Merriam elk was exterminated by 1906. A few sets of antlers and broken skulls are all that remain as evidence of the existence of this "subspecies." However, Yellowstone elk reintroduced into the Merriam elk's old Arizona

1. The **WAPITI (Cervus elaphus canadensis,** Erxleben 1777). This is the largest of the red deer, the most advanced in adaptations to life in open plains and grazing, the best adapted to long winters, and the only one to enter America. Its origin lies in the area of Eastern Siberia and Alaska known as Beringia. From here elk moved east into North America at the time of megafaunal extinction about 12,000 years ago, and west into Siberia, where populations of this subspecies still exist in northern Mongolia, the Altai and Tien Shan mountains. The designation of six subspecies of elk in North America is not tenable since it fails to segregate taxonomically meaningless ecotypes from subspecies.

2. The **MANCHURIAN WAPITI** or **IZBUR STAG (C. e. xanthopygus,** Milne-Edwards 1869) is a forest wapiti, usually much smaller in body size, but particularly in antler size, than our elk. While the males are wapiti-like, the females are red deer-like and have none of the neck mane of our cow elk. It has a very wide distribution, ranging from eastern Mongolia to Yakutia in eastern Siberia, and south to Manchuria and northern China.

3. The **ALSHAN WAPITI (C. e. alashanicus,** Bobrinski and Flerov 1934), found in the mountains rising from the Alashan and Gobi deserts of northern China and southern Mongolia, is the smallest and most conservative wapiti in pelage marking. Little is known about this subspecies, but it appears to have survived in southern Mongolia.

4. The **MacNEILL'S STAG (C. e. macneilli,** Lydekker 1909) is a big highland deer found in eastern Tibet and the mountains of Gansu and Sitchuan provinces of China. The Gansu red deer **(C. e. kansuensis)** has turned out to be identical to MacNeill's deer. Like the elk it is cold-adapted, but unlike the elk it is a saltatorial runner, somewhat mule deer-like in color, ear size, and habitat preference. Life in tall willow and rhododendron thickets on steep slopes below the alpine grasslands makes a jumping mode of locomotion virtually imperative. The majority of stags carry wapiti-like six-pronged antlers.

5. *Another large highland red deer is the* **SHOU** *(C. e. wallichi, Cuvier 1812) of southern Tibet and Butan. It is very rare today. Like the MacNeill's stag, it has long ears, but its body is of different build. It is stocky and appears to be adapted to mountain grasslands, not rhododendron thickets. The antlers are large and of a primitive five-pronged design.*

6. *Almost extinct is the* **KASHMIR STAG** *(C. e. hanglu, Wagner 1844), the most primitive of the red deer. Featuring a five-pronged plan, the antlers have an exceptionally long second tine, while the first tine may erupt rather far up on the beam. The Kashmir stag is smaller than the closely related Shou and MacNeill's stag, and adapted to temperate forests in the foothills of the Himalayas.*

7. *Also close to extinction is the small* **BUCHARA STAG** *(C. e. bactrianus, Lydekker 1900). It is a deer closely tied to dense riparian vegetation of tall reeds and shrubs along desert streams in Turkestan. The stags are colored reminiscent of wapiti, but the antlers are primitive and five-pronged in structure.*

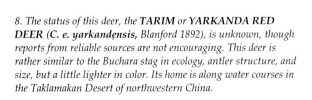

8. *The status of this deer, the* **TARIM** *or* **YARKANDA RED DEER** *(C. e. yarkandensis, Blanford 1892), is unknown, though reports from reliable sources are not encouraging. This deer is rather similar to the Buchara stag in ecology, antler structure, and size, but a little lighter in color. Its home is along water courses in the Taklamakan Desert of northwestern China.*

9. The **EAST EUROPEAN RED DEER** (*C. e. maral,* *Ogilby 1840*) of Turkey, Iran and eastern Europe departs sharply from the red deer considered so far. In European red deer subspecies the antlers of well-developed old males normally have radial branching, forming a "crown." In this deer the crown is least developed. Its antlers and tines tend to be long. It has hybridized extensively with the West European red deer in eastern Europe (below). The subspecific designation of red deer in eastern Europe west of the Black Sea as the separate subspecies **brauneri** is questionable. These can be very large deer, big stags rivalling Rocky Mountain wapiti in size. The hinds are much smaller than the stags.

10. The **WEST EUROPEAN RED DEER** (*C. e. elaphus,* Linnaeus 1758) is much intermixed with other red deer introduced from eastern Europe and Asia, and may disappear entirely with increases in hybridization with feral sika deer. There is uncertainty whether to segregate the Norwegian red deer as a separate subspecies. The North African Barbary stag, designated as the questionable subspecies (*C. e. barbarus*), is also very similar to the West European red deer. Size varies greatly.

11. The **CORSICAN RED DEER** (*C. e. corsicanus,* Erxleben 1777) is so similar in pelage to the west European subspecies that it might be a man-made introduction to the island. It is now confined to Sardinia where a national park is now providing it some badly needed protection.

12. The **SPANISH RED DEER** (*C. e. hispanicus,* Hilzheimer 1909) appears to be a relict form like the Spanish Ibex, the Pyrennean chamois or the Garganta roe deer, similar to forms that inhabited Europe before the great Riss Glaciation. This small deer is in much danger of being displaced by introduced West European red deer.

*A spike bull bolts across open terrain.*
*Elk are better adapted to efficient flight in open plains*
*that any other deer evolved in the Old World.*

mountain haunts have also grown to remarkably large size.

The Manitoba elk, *manitobensis* (Millais, 1915), the elk of the northern prairies and adjacent forests of Manitoba, Saskatchewan and north-central Alberta, may today be the largest-bodied of all elk. A sample of 26 bulls four years of age and over from Elk Island National Park in central Alberta averaged 832 pounds (378 kg) whole weight in early December. That is almost 77 pounds (35 kg) more than equivalent elk from the Rockies in Banff National Park. The heaviest of the 26 bulls weighed 1,034 pounds (470 kg). It was virtually fat-free and would have weighed more than 1,110 pounds (550 kg) whole weight when in good condition in early fall. The average

skull length of this sample of elk was 467 mm. However, two bull elk skulls from Riding Mountain National Park in Manitoba surpass those from Elk Island National Park and are the largest elk skulls measured anywhere. (Roosevelt elk from the Olympic Peninsula transplanted to Afognack Island, Alaska, rival Manitoba elk in size. A fat bull there weighed 1,110 pounds, or 550 kilograms. That is a lot bigger than most bull moose and not far from the expected weight of the fabled Irish elk.)

There is no way I know to distinguish North American elk from Siberian elk living in northern Mongolia and adjacent areas in southern Siberia. Siberian elk have the same type of antlers as our elk, the very same pelage markings, they bugle in the very same fashion,

and they smell like North-American elk. The first Siberian elk I ever saw in captivity initially led me to believe they had been mislabeled by the zoo staff. They had not. They were elk from the Russian part of the Altai Mountains. If one examines hundreds of large antlers of Siberian wapiti, or maral—Europeans prefer to call them by their Mongolian name—one finds a few variants strange to American elk and vice versa. Also, in southern Siberia, east of Lake Baikal, there is some hybridization with Manchurian elk—and consequently, slight oddities in pelage characteristics—but the typical Siberian elk cannot be distinguished from the typical American elk. Since this is so, Siberian and American elk form one single subspecies *Cervus elaphus canadensis* (Erxleben, 1777). I shall refer to them collectively as the *advanced wapiti*.

How is it possible that elk on two continents, thousands of miles apart, are the very same in external characteristics? The answer lies with the geography of late glacial Alaska and eastern Siberia. This was then one land, "Beringia," undivided by the Bering Straits. That division came after deglaciation, about 12,000-9,000 years ago, when the ocean levels rose in response to all the ice melting, flooding central Beringia. The flooding split the Beringia elk population into Siberian and North American ones.

The elk, as a cold-adapted opportunist, did well subsequently in North America only because the competition had died out. Elk were not a part of the rich Pleistocene fauna of North American ecological specialists. That is, elk did not graze alongside

*(Left) Elk, whose origin traces back to the icy landscapes of eastern Siberia and Ice Age Alaska, are very hardy to cold, blizzards and icing. (Below) The death of a forest means the birth of grasslands to which elk will gravitate.*

the Columbian mammoths, the giant peccaries, four-horned prong-horned bucks, North American lamas, and the many primitive species of American horses. The elk had been a member of the "mammoth steppe," according to Dale Guthrie, a famous paleontologist working at the University of Alaska. This "mammoth steppe" stretched from Alaska and the Yukon across the wide Bering Land Bridge to Siberia, and beyond that as far west as Ice Age England. Following the retreat of continental glaciers and the calamitous extinction of the giant American herbivores and carnivores, elk spread as far south as the mountains of northern Mexico, east to the Atlantic, and west to the Pacific shores. So, and not too surprisingly, the same elk are found both in central Asia and throughout North America. Both populations shifted southward, away from the Bering Straits, to occupy eventually the regions they live in today. Like the grizzly bear, timber wolf and the native people of North America, the elk originated in Eurasia and is a recent newcomer to lower North America.

Nor should it surprise us that all American elk are much the same genetically, and distinguishable at best as ecotypes from one another. By that we understand that elk reflect in their morphology and ecology the ecological conditions of the landscape in which they happen to be found.

*(Top left) The growth of antlers begins in bull elk right after shedding. The skin grows rapidly over the antler pedicle once the antlers are dropped. In elk, unlike in mule deer, moose or caribou, the new antler begins growth at once. (Bottom left) The antler buds swell and grow upward, nourished by the bull's stored body resources of energy, protein and minerals. To maximize antler growth, the bull must be in excellent condition one month before shedding antlers.*

## Evolution

Elk are the most highly evolved subspecies of red deer able to cope with open landscapes, coarse-fibred forage and cold climates. Elk are also classical Old World deer, which differ from the other great branch of the deer family, the New World deer (i.e. white-tailed deer and black-tailed deer) in foot structure, brain morphology, skull characteristics, the placement of the penis in males, the pattern of growing and shedding of antlers, and an advertisement strategy by males to attract females. Elk are not only more highly adapted to plains life and cold seasonal climates than any other Old World deer alive, they are the only one of that subfamily ever to set foot in the Americas.

Old World deer, unlike New World deer, left behind an adequate fossil record, and we are fairly well informed about their history on earth. They appear midway through the Tertiary Period (the Age of Mammals), about 35 million years ago. They were small, tropical resource defenders armed with tusk-like fighting canines and small antlers. They also had little endurance when running and needed cover for hiding; without cover, they were quickly caught by predators such as the ancestors of wolves.

From the tropical forests, the primitive Old World deer eventually spread into the tree-studded savannah, then into the treeless steppe, then into cool temperate zones, and from there into high, cold mountains, and finally into the harsh glacial landscapes of the Ice Ages. There was, thus, progressive adaptation to increasingly seasonal climates, which spun off new species.

*(Top right)The bull, while growing antlers, must also grow a new coat of hair. This demands rich forage and access in early summer to mineral licks. (Bottom right) A month away from finishing growth of its antlers, this bull shows he has been a successful forager. Big antlers and a sleek coat of hair are a consequence of high food consumption.*

In the tropics one finds many ecological food specialists. Most have primitive body types. Invariably, they are structured for damaging combat in the defense of food-resources on a territory. Primitive tropical species tend to be not only fighting machines, but are specialized in such fighting that leads to severe damage, usually of both opponents. They use sharp, knife- or dagger-like weapons that generate painful lacerations. The logic of this type of combat is to inflict massive pain on an intruder into a territory, so that it runs off quickly.

In the tropics one finds primitive dwarfs and primitive giants, the former specialized in foraging for small bits of highly digestible, non-toxic vegetation, such as fallen fruit, tender shoots, seeds, and flowers, but also for insects and small animals. These small species have a relatively high metabolic rate, and therefore require rapid digestion of the food; large-bodied forms, having per pound of mass a lower metabolic rate, can feed on fodder that is digested much slower. Therefore, the giants are usually specialists in consuming tough, fibrous, bulk-food.

A the opposite extreme from tropical conditions, in the cold climates around continental glaciers, at high latitude or altitude, one finds the "grotesque giants" of the Pleistocene. They are young species that arose sometime within the Ice Ages, about two million years ago. They are "grotesque" because of oddly shaped "luxury" outgrowths: large and bizarre antlers or horns, heavy fat deposits, and ornate hair coats. They are also large-brained, adaptable ecological generalists. They are, however, poor competitors when faced with warm-climate

*Huge antlers are often somewhat asymmetrical and are carried by bulls in the latter third of their life. Big antlers can grow only on bodies not debilitated by the rutting season and the hardships of the following winter.*

FROM BEYOND SIBERIA 47

relatives and are quite susceptible to the diseases of their southern kin. After all, in cold climates there are few pathogens and parasites to adapt to.

This pattern of geographic dispersal and progressive adaptation to cold climates was repeated by many families of large mammals, primates and man included. Our current human species is cold-adapted, a fat, grotesque giant among primates and comparable to the extinct Irish Elk among Old World deer, or woolly mammoths among elephants.

While the tropics are climatically benign but biologically very stressful, cold climates are biologically benign but climatically very stressful. In the tropics the precious nutrients and minerals are virtually all locked up within the bodies of living plants and animals. Consequently, life there is a struggle for these precious nutrients. This competition leads to ecological specialization in obtaining food. The climate further requires warding off hosts of parasites, pathogens and predators that want to get at those nutrients in living bodies. Evolutionary forces have thus shaped tropical forms to be the smallest size compatible with reproduction and to be territorial defenders of material resources against neighbors. They also have very good immune systems to ward off pathogens and parasites, they store little fat—costly and wasteful to store—and they grow thin hair coats at best, as more is not needed in warm climates. Tropical animals are thus "efficiency" forms, driven to be so by intense competition for limited nutrients.

By contrast, in cold climates food is seasonally superabundant while predators, parasites and pathogens are relatively few and, therefore, much less of a threat. Conversely, low temperature, severe wind chill, icing and difficult snow conditions sap life from a body. In cold regions, though, a summer season ensures every individual a "vacation from want" during which each can grow freely in body size. Some of the summers' surplus is stored as fat, as vitamins in the liver, as minerals in bones to be dissolved for metabolic purposes in winter when good food is scarce, and as protein in a thick dermis, in connective tissue and cell content. Under conditions of superabundance, "luxury tissues" such as heavy fat depots, big antlers or horns, and luxurious hair coats can be grown.

Adaptation to the arctic from the tropics entails profound bodily, ecological and behavioral changes. One cannot be an ecological specialist in seasonal climates, which proffer ever-changing types of food. One must be able to change. The food may also be in the open or in cover, forcing one to have a diversity of strategies to deal with predators. Grouping is a fine anti-predator strategy in the open, but it requires getting along with one's neighbors, a difficult feat for a tropical, territory-defending, intolerant species. One expression of this evolution in cold-adapted mammals is their large brains.

Old World deer had many lineages that evolved in temperate and cold climates into gregarious open-country forms. The red deer species is but the latest such radiation. Red deer originated

The succulent, growing portions of plants, such as the white meristem of the cattail pulled out by this cow elk, contain much of the sugars, proteins, vitamins and minerals needed to produce the rich milk required by the calf.

FROM BEYOND SIBERIA        49

from ancestors similar to sika deer (*Cervus nippon*, Temminck 1837). Sikas are still very much with us. They range from small, subtropical subspecies in Vietnam and southern China to rather big-bodied, cold-adapted races in Manchuria and Hikkaido. A small-bodied sika inhabits much of Japan, while various Japanese islands contain unique subspecies with yet smaller body size.

Compared with red deer, with which they can hybridize, sika deer are not only smaller, they are less well adapted to cold and snow, though better adapted to warm climates. They are much more bound to cover than are red deer, and are saltatorial runners with very little endurance. In the rut, sikas show strong territorial tendencies. As expected from subtropical ancestors, sika deer are more specialized to digest fibrous forage than are red deer, and are also very hardy to diseases.

Red deer probably originated in the foothills of the Himalayas, from where they spread latitudinally and altitudinally to colonize increasingly more-open, cold landscapes. The common red deer of Europe is the West-European red deer, *C. e. elaphus* (Linnaeus, 1758). It is a dark form with a well developed neck mane, a dark belly, a light face and relatively short antlers with multiple terminal branches forming a "crown."

The advanced wapiti of Asia and America, our elk, differ from other forms of red deer in having larger antlers, a strongly contrasting coat with the largest rump patch and the shortest tail, larger teeth, and a preference for open landscapes. In Asia, they are confined to cold mountain grasslands and subalpine forests, while primitive Manchurian wapiti and red deer occupy the forested lowlands. However, all subspecies of red deer feature distinct rutting calls, that of advanced wapiti being a high-pitched bugle, selected for long-distance communication.

Our elk, then, is a red deer—albeit the largest, the most highly evolved for running and grazing, and thus best adapted to life in open plains. It is the most colorful and the most widespread geographically of any of the red deer's recognized subspecies. It is also a product of adaptations to glacial dynamics, the rise and fall of sea levels, and the consequent shifts in climatic zones.

SURVIVAL AND THE HERD

*Elk are highly evolved for swift running in uneven terrain. Calf elk, after a brief period of hiding following birth, must soon be able to follow their dam with speed and endurance.*

Security from predation is the supreme concern of elk. It shapes them directly and indirectly. We noted that the elk, of all the Old World deer, is the most highly evolved for swift, sustained running. Yet it is not quite as swift as a fine horse bred for speed and endurance. However, the elk will outrun the fine horse the moment it dodges into cover, marshes or rough terrain. The elk's abilities at running are but a part of an interrelated complex of security, social and ecological adaptations. This complex has evolved repeatedly among other horned ungulates that make their home in open landscapes.

Central to this adaptive complex, and therefore to elk biology, is to join with others into a "selfish herd" for security. The herd is labeled "selfish" because, even though joining with others, each member of the herd is still looking out for itself. Life in a herd has many ramifications: Each individual must get along with its companions; females must be able to withstand competition from the young males in their company; because predators are free to pursue the herd, the running ability of the herd members must be superb; the young must soon be able to run as fast and enduring as their mothers; with nowhere to hide, silence and stealth is abandoned in favor of a noisy, showy and often smelly social life. Also, and counter-intuitively, female-choice in mating begins to assert supremacy over male despotism, forcing males to advertise in courtship. The elk is well along in all these adaptations, an unusual condition for deer; only the caribou and the great Irish Elk, now extinct, went further.

While bison, antelope and horses have readily taken to open plains and life in big herds, such is not the case for deer. They are tied closely to woody and herbaceous vegetation, which excludes them from grassy steppes and deserts but not the tundra. The reason is probably the inordinate requirement deer have for minerals for antler growth. Compared to foliage and browse, grasses, while adequate in protein, are relatively poor in calcium and phosphates. An elk could not eat enough grass to grow normal antlers. It must find foliage, such as willow leaves, rich in bone-building minerals (calcium, phosphate) to supplement a diet of grasses and sedges. Antelope, which grow no bony antlers but instead sport horns grown from protein, can afford a diet almost exclusively of grasses. As we shall see, elk, relative to their large body size, carry quite small antlers. That may be due in part to their diet high in grasses and sedges. How elk lived in huge herds on the coverless, dry plains of the immense central valley of California in centuries past, we shall never know. However, the antlers of these elk were neither long nor massive.

*The bull elk, to grow large antlers, must find adequate amounts of foliage rich in protein and minerals. A diet of grasses will not do.*

Any runner, to convert energy efficiently to propulsion, must reduce costly body-lift. This decreases the up and down motions of the body during each foot-fall cycle. The less the center of gravity is displaced upward, the more energy is directed to forward propulsion, and the lower the cost per unit of horizontal distance moved, the longer the animal can run on its stored energy.

Such locomotion is only possible where there are few obstructions that force the animal to

(Left) Wounded and weakening, this elk's fate is sealed. Escape into water only delays the inevitable. Demanding winter weather drains the meager body stores of young elk, dulls their attention and slows their flight. Elk, despite their large size, are notoriously inept at fighting off predators. (Below) A coyote "casing" a herd of elk, checking systematically and often for weak, inattentive or disabled individuals.

jump or to lift its legs to great height. Thus, "cursors," as speedy runners are called technically, can evolve only where the ground cover, relative to their length of legs, is low — where the land is level and where there are few obstructions to impede steady running. The extreme condition is, of course, flat desert. Here we also find the extreme in cursorial adaptation: the short-legged cursors such as saiga antelope, addax or gemsbucks. Short legs lessen body lift, and short steps even out locomotion. Short-legged cursors run with their head low. They can afford to — there are virtually no obstructions to worry about. Long-legged cursors, evolved to speedy running over uneven ground, run with an elevated head — as do pronghorn bucks, dama gazelles, argali sheep, and of course, our elk.

The three most important advantages for elk in a selfish herd are the "dilution effect," the "position effect," and the "weaker neighbor effect." The "dilution effect" refers to the chances of being caught by a predator when alone as opposed to being in a group. A lone elk on the open plain has a hungry wolf pack's undivided attention. However, when the elk is surrounded by a thousand others, the chances of it being singled out by a predator are a thousandfold less. The bigger the herd, the lower the chances of each elk being singled out for the kill.

The "position effect" compounds the dilution effect for the individual within the herd. Because predators take prey from the edge of a herd, an individual in the center of the herd is

virtually safe from predation. The bigger the herd of elk, the lower the proportion of elk that form the periphery relative to the number of elk within the herd. That's a consequence of the geometry of a circle; big herds are safer than small herds.

The "weaker neighbor effect" labels the chance that when running from a predator within a herd, there will be someone slower who then gets caught. This makes the herd a dangerous place for the ill, the old, the disabled or the heavily pregnant. Not surprisingly, such individuals withdraw from the herd because in flight they are guaranteed to be left behind and become victims of the predators. A healthy elk of average ability in the middle of a large herd in the open plains,

however, is virtually immune to predation.

Some other advantages suggested for herd life, such as the likelihood of many eyes seeing predators more readily, turn out to be inconsequential on closer inspection. At night all those watchful eyes are of little help. The noise of the herd and clouds of herd-scent drown out the noise and scent of approaching predators. At night, when predators are most active, the herd is relatively easy to locate due to its scent and noise. Yet, the prey animals remain in a herd.

To live in a herd, the individuals must get along with one another. When fights break out, weapons must not inflict wounds. If they do, the winner and the loser will both attract the

*In herd-forming ruminants, horns and antlers evolve to permit parrying and wrestling. The latter is central to the friendly sparring matches of bulls before and after the rutting season.*

attention of predators. Unlike much human aggression, in which an aggressor can instantly disable his victim with a lethal weapon such as a club, sword or gun, the aggressor in animal societies is likely to be wounded due to retaliation by the defender. Weapons carried by deer or antelope can inflict lethal wounds, but they cannot normally disable an opponent instantly as can a human weapon. Victory in combat can be rather hollow if the winner's bleeding wounds make him subject to increased attention by predators. While he has won a battle, he may have lost the war. Wounded, he cannot persevere in a selfish herd. It is not to his advantage to trigger in his opponent a desperate defense with sharp weapons that break his own skin. Consequently, social life in the selfish herd requires a change in weaponry,

from the short, sharp weapons typical of primitive territorial resource defenders to weapons that allow a new type of fighting: wrestling, a test of strength with a minimum external injury.

Despite their many differences, most complex antelope horns and deer antlers have something in common: They are configured to allow a grip on the other fellow's horns or antlers in a wrestling match. Also, the spreading horns or antlers allow the defender to catch and hold the attack of the aggressor. That is, spreading antlers can be used to parry the opponent's blow, as in fencing. Furthermore, by binding the aggressor's antlers, the defender temporarily deactivates the aggressor's ability to thrust again. As long as

the defender can hang on to the aggressor's antlers with his own, he enjoys a temporary safety from the opponent's weapon. But binding antlers allows both to test their strength against one another in wrestling. The force exerted by one animal against the other may convince the weaker to choose an appropriate moment to disengage and run. The maneuver to separate is dangerous, however, for the winner can gore the turning loser in the side or hindquarters when he retreats, or bowl him over and gore him repeatedly.

Thus, in bull elk, not too surprisingly, wounds are located primarily about the head and neck and again on the rear end. A bull collects about fifty wounds per mating season, some of which can be quite severe. In this type of fighting, obviously, only the loser is likely to get a serious wound—when he turns to run and thus cannot retaliate. There is thus no cost to the aggressor when he wounds a retreating subordinate.

Another result of this new, stereotyped form of fighting is the evolution of "sporting matches," or sparring, between antlered males. This is, in the long course of mammalian evolution, a relatively new form of behavior. Sparring allows the males to learn about one another without anyone losing rank or "face." It's also great for learning about one's own headgear. Further, it provides some practice in fighting and trains the appropriate muscles. It is a controlled, harmless outlet for aggression and can be used to form

*The possession of complex antlers is linked to the common sporting engagements between bulls, the sparring matches. In these matches neither partner gains or loses rank, but each is able to learn the dimensions of its rack as well as the agility and power of prospective rivals.*

"friendships" between stags. Sparring stags can thus have "fun" with one another, yet each retains its respective rank, even though the bigger may give way in a contest.

Elk advertise that they are merely sparring by yelping loudly. Potential sparring partners also approach one another with raised heads and slow steps to engage antlers as if on command. That is a "symmetrical" match in which each stag plays "dominant." This is quite different from the asymmetrical sparring matches of white-tailed or mule deer. In those species the smaller deer uses behaviors appropriate of the subordinate, the larger deer behaviors appropriate of the dominant. Yet sparring is pure "sport" in all cases.

Now comes a complex chain of reasons that explains why, in elk and red deer, antlers are so much larger than in other deer of similar size. Curiously, the chain of logic begins not with antlers but with the newborn calf. A calf is small, defenseless against predators, cannot run fast enough to save its life, and depends entirely on its mother for nutrition. How is it safeguarded?

To safeguard their offspring, all deer except the caribou have behaviors designed to hide the calf, or even hide occasionally with the calf, as do moose. Hiding is a very effective way to reduce contact between predators and newborns. As long as the calf hides, it is fairly well protected. However, the mothers of hidden calves are bound to an area as long as the calves are in hiding; they cannot use the vastness of open country to escape predators. Therefore, the mother's safety demands that, as soon as possible, the young be able use their legs and run as fast and as enduring as the mother. This

*Elk calves hide in their first few days of life by crouching motionless in whatever cover they happen to find. Even their body odors are minimal at this age, and predators may wander past without scenting them.*

SURVIVAL AND THE HERD 67

can be done by carrying the young in the uterus until it is large and sufficiently well developed so that it can run fast within minutes of being born—as in the African wildebeest—or it means decreasing the calf's hiding period by supplying it with a lot of milk as rich in energy, protein, and minerals as possible, to facilitate rapid growth. This predicts that the more a species is adapted to life in the open, coverless plains, the larger or the better developed its young must be at birth. And that is what we find, including in the elk. The elk calf at birth is relatively large, and it does not stay in hiding as long as, say, the fawn of white-tailed deer. Moreover, to give birth to large young precludes raising twins or triplets. Dividing nutrients and energy between two or three young in the uterus would mean the young would be born too small to mature quickly into capable runners. Consequently, most ungulates who are year-round residents of open plains not only have large or well-developed young at birth, they also normally give birth to only one offspring. And that applies also to elk.

The richer the milk, the greater the growth of the calf. That should make the milk of elk rich in solids, and it is. Because of dangers from predators close to waterholes, though, this rule may be contravened by species from areas where water is scarce and highly localized. In such cases the mother's milk must be the carrier of water to the young. Consequently, the milk in some large steppe and desert dwellers, whose young at birth are huge, may be surprisingly "dilute." This is the case in horses or camels. Where water is abundant and readily available, such as on the barren grounds, the milk solids reach their highest value, namely in

*Calf elk run to their mothers for suckling and are recognized individually by their scent. Elk must give birth to large calves and produce rich milk to shorten the period when the calf is small and very vulnerable to predators. This demands single births so that all effort is put into bearing a large, well-developed calf. Suckling is of long duration in elk, as cows visit their hidden calves relatively infrequently.*

*Symmetry of antlers speaks for a bull's robust health, massive size for superior foraging ability, and an efficient, frugal maintenance of the body. That's the female's ideal for a father for daughters that must produce large calves and rich milk.*

caribou. (Note: where the mother can hide separately from the newborn young in thickets, where there is no pressure to use space for safety, there is no need for large young, or well-developed young, or rich milk to speed development, or a short hiding period for the young. Nor is there a restriction of bearing several young. That's what has shaped the white-tailed deer, compared with the elk.)

What has all this to do with antlers in males? If the mother is to produce big babies and rich milk, she must be able to divert to her young a relatively large amount of energy and nutrients from her own body's growth and maintenance. She must lessen her own needs and size to apply it to the growth of the child. Being a good mother, she would want her daughters to be as good or better at raising big babies. Therefore, she would search for a father with abilities to divert nutrients from his body growth towards reproduction, abilities that are as good or better than her own.

But how does a cow elk find a father with superior abilities at sparing nutrients from maintenance towards reproduction?

This is where "luxury organs," including antlers, come in. To grow large antlers, a bull elk must be very good at finding superior forage in large quantities, and he must be able to spare a lot of nutrients and energy from his body growth and maintenance. However, to do that, he must be masterly at avoiding illness, injury, and costly exertions. He must be efficient in the budgeting of his "income." Large antlers are signs of an efficient forager and a frugal user of ingested nutrients. Moreover, the symmetry of antlers is proof of health. The healthier the bull, the fewer parasites it has, the fewer the diseases that infect it, the fewer the injuries it must heal, the more symmetrical its antlers. Therefore, a big bull with large, symmetrical antlers is living proof of his own success as a forager, as an efficient converter of food to tissue, and of his superior abilities in staying out of trouble. That's the father the cow wants for her children! If he can also face the challenges of scrappy rivals, he is a candidate as a herd bull. To our eyes, such a bull would be an awesome, beautiful fellow, and chances are that that's just how cow elk see it too. There is evidence that large mammals happen to have the same perceptual mechanisms as we do and fall for symmetry as much as do humans. Symmetry, a proxy for health, is a vital attribute of what we consider beauty, be it symmetry in shape or symmetry in motion or symmetry in sound.

This thinking predicts that species with small antlers would give birth to relatively small young, and vice versa. And that is indeed found. Also, species with large antlers should have richer milk, and they do. Moreover, we would expect males in species with large antlers would use these luxury growth symbols as advertisements when they court females. This is also found. The reason why horns and antlers in plains-adapted antelope and deer do not always grow large is because with many of these species it is not a male's body but his "real estate," his possession of a mating territory, that is attractive to females. In territorial species the antlers are strictly tools for fighting and do not serve as organs of advertisement.

(Note: In elk, which roam over large areas and

*(Left) Bulls, to succeed in the mating game, must grow large. To do so, they search out rich forage and take chances with predators, but still form "selfish" herds whenever possible. (Bottom left) Cow elk, to protect their calves, concede food quality in favor of the security of large herds in open terrain.*

are found in many different habitats that impose different demands on individuals, the female can rely on antler size and symmetry to track the genetics of success of potential mates. Different genes and gene combinations are expected to become prominent in different environments. Luxury organs and symmetry always track biological success and genetic adaptedness within a given landscape. No matter how varied the environment, large, symmetrical antlers track the success of bulls. As long as females choose males with large, symmetrical antlers, they ensure a superior combination of genes for their children — a combination likely to differ from region to region.)

Granted the foregoing, one can explain another attribute of elk biology: the segregation of males from females during all but the mating season. Most of the year, one finds cow elk in large groups, but large bull elk form small groups or are quite frequently alone. Young bulls may be found with either the female groups or with the males.

This segregation arises due to the different objectives of the sexes: Females maximize the security of calves at the expense of food, bulls maximize growth and development at the expense of security. To succeed biologically, bulls need to be large in body and antler size, so it is imperative that they search for the very best food. Since bulls are large and good runners, they can take chances with predators that would be fatal to calves.

Cow elk, in contrast to bulls, need not maximize nutrient intake to ensure biological success. In fact, increasing food intake late in pregnancy could be fatal to the cow and the unborn calf at birth. Very large calves are expected to bring about complications at birth, become stuck in the birth canal or die of dystocia — the technical term for crushing the calf through the birth canal. Painful births may also cause females to desert their calf. So, very large calves are a double jeopardy because they may not be viable and may cause the death of the female as well.

Small calves are also not viable as they may cool down too rapidly at birth and fail to generate enough body heat to survive cold spring weather. Moreover, they are not likely to reach a size large enough by fall to survive the rigors of winter. Thus the best strategy for the female is to bear a calf neither too large nor to small — that is, to *optimize* birth weight.

Yet a male, to succeed, must maximize growth. So, the bull elk cannot afford to be with cow elk if they are on food adequate for optimizing birth weight. He must find better food or else fail reproductively in competition with other bulls. Females can graze down a range and still do well reproductively. But this makes it impossible for bulls to be with them if better foraging is available elsewhere. So, after bull elk colonize an area previously unoccupied by elk, they will leave it for other ranges once the females arrive and take over.

In practice, the segregation of cows and bulls leaves females in larger groups on open, grassy plains while bulls move into small clearings in forests, into cuts made by creeks and rivers, or into areas where wildfires have removed climax forests. These bull-occupied habitats provide vegetation rich in forbs and woody plants. Bulls are also likely to wander more, be alone, and hide in timber and undergrowth instead of grouping with others in the open.

*(Left) Growing, blood-engorged antlers spell food for biting flies, and torment for the elk. (Below) Following the rut, some bulls take a chance on high elevation and deep snow to escape predation, but may succumb to the elements in hard winters.*

Another influence segregating bulls from cows is the exhaustion and wounding bulls suffer during the rutting season. Not only are the bulls then debilitated by the loss of fat stores and many antler wounds that need to heal, they are also hampered by injuries that impair speedy and enduring running. Due to their large size and big antlers, however, they are as conspicuous as sore thumbs. The association of large antlers with weakened prey would quickly teach predators that large-antlered elk, compared with antlerless elk or those with only small antlers, are easy to catch. To escape notice by predators, then, rutted-out bulls, until they regain a semblance of their pre-rut abilities, must avoid female company. So, exhausted bulls hide and move to areas where snow-depth, for instance, gives them some advantage over the shorter-legged wolves. Here, too, finding the bulls would cost the predators more energy than a kill would repay.

Another complexity of herding behavior is how cows deal with competition for food from young bulls that stay in the herd. Cows have responded to such competition, through evolution, by growing close to the body size and aggressive abilities of young bulls. That is, the females evolve via male mimicry — a universal response by females in species of ungulates that form big herds. This rule is illustrated nowhere better than by female barren-ground caribou. When female caribou

dig a large hole in the deep snow to feed on
lichens, they must watch out for young bulls
ever ready to pirate their costly work. Young
bulls, unless confronted, will displace cows and
feed on lichens exposed by the labor of the
females, but caribou females have just the right
antler and body size to stand off young bulls.

Compared with the ancestral red deer, elk have
reduced, but not eliminated, the differences in
size and external appearance of the sexes. While
red deer females are about half the mass of the
mature males and feature no neck mane as the
males do, female elk are exceeded in mass by
old bulls only 1.2-1.4 times. Also, cows carry big
neck manes. Moreover, on the front of elk
skulls, where bulls grows the antler pedicles,
one sees in female elk, but not in female red
deer, a little bone outgrowth. It is a mini-pedicle
without antlers. Antlered cow elk, moreover,
are not the rarity they are among red deer.

The decision by ancestral red deer and
their even more gregarious descen-
dants, the wapiti, to unite in large
herds for protection from predators has had far-
reaching ramifications. It accounts for the rich
social life of elk, enhanced advertisement by
courting bulls, large young at birth, the rarity of
multiple births, large antlers, ornateness of the
coat, a body form adapted to running, and the
reduced physical distinction between the sexes.

*Coyotes, magpies and ravens are the clean-up crew that removes
dead elk, no matter how they died. These remains are of an elk that
broke its front legs while crossing a frozen river. Grizzly bears,
efficient predators on calves and occasionally on adult elk, scavenge
winter-killed elk right after emerging from hibernation, a time
when plant food is not yet available and the bears must husband
the last of their fat deposits.*

RUTTING ELK

*The bugling of bull elk signals the commencement of the rut, the most dramatic event in the annual cycle of elk. Bugling is advertising. It is attractive to cows but signals to other bulls the caller's readiness to fight.*

In that craggy spine of North America, the Rocky Mountains, the bugling of bull elk is expected to reverberate in the mountain valleys sometime in late August. That sound signals the beginning of a significant annual event, the mating season of elk. It sparks the start of intense, dramatic activity. Elk begin again the ancient process of renewing their species, testifying to an unbroken string of renewals going back millions and millions of years. The rut is dramatic for good reasons. This brief time of the year is when the winners in the reproductive game are winnowed from the losers. And elk put all they have into trying to be winners.

The timing of the rut is critical. Should a female ovulate and come into heat too early, her newborn calf will die in the cold, snow, and storms of late winter. If a female ovulates too late, her calf will be born after the peak of nutritious spring growth of plants, too late to receive a full milk supply, too late to grow to survivable size before the harsh winter sets in — it becomes ready prey of grizzly, wolf or mountain lions. Conversely, a bull that enters the rut too early wastes the precious store of fat he accumulated in summer on futile herding and courting. He is a loser, as is a bull that enters the rut too late.

The timing of the rut is determined in general by the best season for the survival, growth, and development of the calf. In cold-temperate climates, at high latitudes and altitudes, this is late spring, when the sprouting forage offers abundant, palatable, non-toxic food. The shorter

*There is a long, drawn-out, high-pitched component to the bugle,
designed by nature to carry great distances, plus a deep-chested
roar advertising the bull's size, and a "chuckle" associated
with urine-spraying.*

the spring, the shorter and more intense the rutting season must be. Consequently, elk in southern parts of their range, such as those in California, rut longer than do elk in Alberta.

The environmental factor that initiates the rut is the decreasing amount of daylight per twenty-four hours after the summer solstice. Day length affects the hormonal clocks of elk. A succession of increasingly shorter days signals elk that they must prepare for the rut, and they do. Light stimulates, through the eye, the lower part of the brain stem (the hypothalamus) and the

pituitary gland, where the hormonal control center over reproduction resides.

Granted birth in spring, the rutting date is then set by the length of pregnancy, or gestation period, of the female. Since gestation period increases with body size, large-bodied deer such as elk or moose rut earlier than do small-bodied deer such as mule and white-tailed deer. Elk rut particularly early and have a noticeably longer gestation period than red deer of similar size. This characteristic the elk shares with a fellow traveler from the

*Elk breed in harems. These are closely guarded by harem bulls against rivals, as well as for escapes by cows.*

abodes of ancient Siberia, the mountain sheep of North America. We suspect the long gestation period has something to do with long, hard glacial winters in Ice Age Beringia. That is, severe shortages of food, great cold and wind chill over a longer winter than today selected for female elk that gave priority to their own bodily needs over those of a growing young. They simply grew the young more slowly, extending the gestation period.

The rut in elk is much more spectacular than in mule deer, white-tailed deer, caribou or moose.

This is because the elk rut is based squarely on male advertisement. Bull elk go out of their way to advertise their worth to maintain a harem of females. By contrast, a buck deer searches out and breeds a succession of does dispersed within his territory. So does a bull moose, ably assisted by cow moose that may call loudly, advertising their presence and receptiveness. Receptive female white-tailed deer get the same effect by going on a long runs through the countryside, driving bucks they encounter into hot pursuit and severe competition. That selects

*(Left) Crooked, asymmetrical antlers grow mostly on old bulls such as this fellow who is blind in one eye and injured in the other. He badly injured and infected the far right antler when in velvet, thus resulting in the malformation.*

out quickly the able runners from the slow ones, and the strong and resourceful bucks from the weak and the meek. It must work well, for whitetails are the oldest species of deer in the world, having been around for some four million years or more.

Advertising shapes everything in a bull elk's life. His antler size tells at a glance of his success at foraging. The symmetry of his antlers reflects the bull's health, as crooked antlers grow on sick, parasitized, senile or injured bulls. The volume and pitch of the bull's voice determines how far he can be heard; high sounds in unobstructed terrain carry farther than low ones. The depth of his grunt indicates his body size; the deeper the sound, the bigger the chest that made it. The amount of rut scent he produces by spraying urine on his belly reveals his level of self-confidence. Only capable, confident bulls horn trees often, spray urine copiously, and wallow frequently; intimidated bulls do little of this. So, big bulls spray more urine on their belly, chest and neck mane, roll more frequently in their urine-soaked wallows and, through horning

*(Top left) Rutting bulls perfume themselves by spraying urine on their bodies, in particular into the long hairs on their belly and neck. Bulls may aim streams of urine between their front legs with great precision, hitting themselves in the neck. (Bottom left) Bulls rub their urine-soaked necks on trees, thereby dispensing their individual scent for the benefit of the harem.*

and neck-rubbing trees, distribute more of their scent than do insecure rivals. (The "chuckle" at the end of the big bull's bugle goes hand in hand with the twitching of the belly, which one can see even at some distance. That's when the bull sprays urine.)

Urine spraying by bull elk has evolved to high virtuosity. While a bull elk cannot coil his penis in snake-like fashion to the side of the body, look backward and spray a urine jet into its face—as can the great sambar stags of India—the bull elk's range of performance is remarkable enough. He can hit with the bundled urine stream his lowered chin, aiming forward between his front legs. At the other extreme, he can let go with a cone of urine mist. The tip of his penis is structured to allow voluntary control over the shape and aim of the urine stream. The urine is sponged up by his belly hair and long neck mane.

Bull elk dig wallows into which they urinate. They dig up the soil with their antlers and roll in the urine-soaked mud. They rub their long-haired necks on the edges of their wallows. Then they transfer the urine by rubbing their muddy necks on trees, as do virtually all large deer species. Rutting bull elk do not feed much, but they do drink plenty of water. Instead of eating, they burn their large fat stores, laid down from the excesses of summer, to free as much time as possible to attend to searching, herding, courting, and breeding. As a result, the big bulls are destined to grow very slim over the course of little more then a month.

Prime bulls advertise their presence with a loud, distinct voice, by distributing scent and by

*Bulls preferentially horn young trees during agonistic engagements. Only very confident bulls, "bullies" willing to fight, test their opponents by horning trees.*

*(This page) Bull elk wallow during the rut. They prepare wallows by urinating, then pawing and horning the soil. Bulls roll in their wallows, covering their bodies and especially their long-haired necks with scented soil. (Right) Rising from a wallow, this big bull has picked up a bunch of dead, muddy vegetation, and appears to be deliberately carrying it about, as if showing off.*

*(Left) Rutting bull elk feed very little, but they drink plenty of water. (Below) Confident bulls show off to others by vigorously horning the ground, tearing out chunks of grass and sod, scattering it widely. Such a demonstration may be the prelude to a fight or to chasing off a rival.*

making themselves conspicuous. The aim: to attract females whose movements they will control and which they will hold in harems.

Controlling female movements within a harem is part of a bull's insurance policy, at best, for cows can and do escape herding bulls. A herd bull must rely on advertisement to hold females, otherwise he loses them to rivals that advertise better than he does. Thus, the herd bull must become for the cows the smallest evil. From the cow's perspective, the greater evils are the lesser bulls. Lesser bulls impatiently try at every opportunity to run down unprotected, frightened females. The female, then, enjoys at least some protection from such harassment by staying close to the big herd bull. Here the impatient youngsters do not dare venture. Here a cow may have some peace, but she must expect to be tested periodically by the big brute, the herd bull itself. That brute, however, employs system in his courtship.

A cow elk, clearly, has to deal with the bull in two very different situations: The first is when she ventures beyond the harem's range and triggers "herding" by the bull, the second when the bull tests her for sexual receptivity. In the first instance, the bull herds her back to his harem, and he is perfectly brutish about it. He trots rapidly ahead of the cow, cuts her off and aids her speedy return to the harem by aggressively rushing her. He may strike her with his antlers, and cow elk do carry antler wounds to prove it. Clearly, herding is a frightening, painful experience to the cow, one that aims at teaching her to avoid moving from the group.

*Bulls race ahead of cows departing the harem to cut off their escape route, then herd them back to the harem. Young bulls, eager to court, may harass cows severely unless stopped by the herd bull, who, by keeping them away, ensures peace for the harem.*

*(Left) When conditioning his harem, a bull may copiously lick individual cows, particularly when the females are at rest. (Below) A courted female moves from the bull in a head-low posture. She may rapidly work her jaws and twist her head, a signal to the bull to terminate courting. The herd bull obeys, then turns and bugles, reinforcing the courted cow's experience of control with the signature of his voice.*

If the bull is to test the cow for sexual receptivity, however, he clearly cannot approach her in a herding posture. The courting bull does not. He uses the sexual approach, showing the exact opposite posture, movements, and sounds to the herding approach.

The bull emphasizes as much as he can through these signals his peaceful, seductive intentions. Instead of circling the cow as in aggressive herding, he approaches her directly in the sexual advance. Instead of stretching his neck low and laying back his antlers, he raises his neck and antlers. He also lets the cow know

exactly what he will do, once he reaches her, by flicking his tongue in and out, a signal that he will copiously lick her. And he does just that, provided he reaches her.

A cow may not be too willing to be tested by the bull, or she may be deeply frightened and run off. While doing so she does something that is very important: She holds her head low, weaves and twists it from side to side, and opens and closes her mouth rapidly. That's her "stop" signal to the bull.

And the big brute does stop! Then he turns around and bugles *away from* the female. He thus allows her to be "in control." Psychologically, it must be some relief for the cow elk to be able to stop the big bull. He reinforces her "success" by his distinctive personal bugle. That is, the cow begins to associate with *his* voice her ability to control him. His advertisement should thus carry a positive meaning for her. No hasty young bull could or would do this. A young bull would pursue the cow no matter how much she signaled for him to stop. For her, his voice would be only cause for alarm.

Spike bulls have no easy time of being spike bulls during the rut. Small though they may be, they now get their first taste of what being a bull elk is all about. Summer in the cow herds was a fine time for them, for some a very fine time. For a lucky few, their second summer was one still attached to apron strings. They not only followed mommy, but mommy even allowed them to suckle.

The first time I saw that, a herd of elk was lazing in July on a grassy slope above our patrol cabin deep within Banff National Park. From old habit, I raised the spotting scope to scan and count the

*Young bulls, satellites to the harem, watch constantly for an opportunity to move in and herd off a cow or to breed an unattended female. They are quick to answer rivals of equal size as well as to test strangers, and they will exploit every weakness shown by a harem bull.*

RUTTING ELK     105

animals. I had just focused on a large cow calmly feeding in the lush green when a huge spike bull walked alongside her, dropped to his knees, and, in suckling, almost lifted the cow off the ground. Did she mind? Not one bit. She even turned and licked his neck and withers.

That young bull had unusually long antlers. They were only spikes, but spikes that seemed to grow forever. I do not know what he could have done with them, except broken them off in the first round of fighting. Spike antlers do occasionally break off, sometimes even at the base. That is not too surprising since the pedicles are rather thin in a bull elk sporting his first antlers. With age the pedicles grow in diameter, becoming better bases for fighting, but in spike bulls they are thin. Given poor nutrition, skulls are thin, light and translucent, and antler breakage is likely. Conversely, with good nutrition the skull bones are dense and the antlers have a thick, ivory-hard cortex, while the amount of central spongy bone is reduced.

As the rut approaches, spike bulls are in trouble. When the big bulls make their rounds, the spikes are chased off. There is no place for them in the harems. The spikes are on their own, chased out by larger bulls. Several spikes may join into a small group and move about, but they are fearful, always ready to run.

A consequence of the bull elk's system of personal advertisement during the rut is that cow elk need have neither a showy urination posture nor a showy heat period as one sees in estrous whitetail or mule deer does. A cow elk urinates in much the same posture as the bull,

so the female urination posture carries little significance for bull elk.

Nor is there any point to a showy display of heat within the harem. A showy heat could fire up rival bulls who would then disrupt the harem. After all, advertisement by the bulls implies female choice. Once the female has chosen, it is not to her advantage to be bred by a different bull. Currently, that's our suspicion, for female choice in elk has yet to be conclusively demonstrated. There is, though, plenty of circumstantial evidence that it does take place.

A bull's aim, clearly, must be to breed as many females as possible. The earlier he begins advertising, the more females he can "convince" of his ability to provide effective shelter from harassment from young bulls, while teaching the cows that they are "in control." The more he advertises, the fewer females are likely to leave him, attracted and made curious about other actively bugling bulls. Consequently, the frequency of bugling coincides with the greatest amount of female activity. Also, it is in the bull's interest to out-advertise other bulls or to shut them up if it is in his power to do so. Thus, an advertising rival who happens to be nearby will be sought out and aggressively silenced. That's why bugling attracts bulls.

A disadvantage of advertising, from the bull's perspective, is that the more successful he is, the more likely he will attract rivals. His harem is a prize worth fighting for, and bull elk are none too shy about fighting. The collective antler

wounds on their bodies, often exceeding fifty per rutting season, indicate that much. Wounds may cause problems after the rutting season, for the many wounds inflicted by dirty, urine-smeared antlers have to heal. No wonder that after the rut big bull elk may resemble little more than a pitiful heap of hide-covered bones.

When a large rival approaches the harem, the herd bull may have to submit to the ultimate test: He may have to fight. Fighting, however, is not heedlessly engaged in by either contestant. To convince the other to quit rather than fight is a worthwhile goal, and both bulls act as if they have that goal in mind. They begin the engagement by "showing off" to one another, bull elk style. They bugle at each other. They approach one another only to stop and vigorously smash small trees with their antlers. That is a powerful, intimidating signal, as I discovered when using a cast elk antler to "horn" trees. I have thus inadvertently intimidated small bulls that I approached in cover. A bull that bugles, smashes trees and urine sprays simultaneously is a dangerous bully!

When the two contesting bulls come close, they quickly vie for the "uphill position" for fighting. The uphill position has the advantage of gravity, and once a bull gains the momentum in shoving the rival downhill, he has virtually won. The two big bulls may continue their "showing off" by walking or even trotting side by side, back and forth across the hillside. These parallel runs may cover up to 300 paces at a stretch. The bulls continue to bugle at one another, stop to smash

*Dominance fights, in which bulls exert themselves and may wound one another, are not common, and are usually short in duration. However, matched bulls may also get involved in lengthy fights, some with fatal consequences. Severely damaging fights are not in the interest of either bull, for long fights are exhausting and predispose both bulls to predation. A danger point for the loser is disengagement, when the winner may pounce quickly forward and gore him in the side or in the rump.*

trees with their antlers, spray urine in shows of supreme confidence during the parallel march, and tilt antlers at one another.

It appears to me, judging from captive bulls and their manner of attack, that the charge is provoked if one bull catches the other opponent off guard. That is, the moment one is off guard, the other charges. However, charges are normally met by the attacked bull catching the opponent's rush with its antlers. Displaying bulls clearly do need to pay attention.

After the bulls lock antlers, a match of bodily strength begins, which, even if it lasts only minutes, can exhaust the combatants. Real fights are usually short. The weaker, in giving up, must find a way to disengage safely, because if he turns and runs, he exposes his body to attack and mortal danger. Winning bulls are not reluctant to gore a fleeing rival. Usually the loser can turn so quickly at an opportune moment that the winner is unable to thrust his antler points into the loser's side, and may only reach his rump. The winner, after pouncing after the loser and bellowing at him with the pursuit call, stops and bugles after the departed rival. The loser in turn may stop and bugle back, bruised and defeated, but not broken. This is what usually happens. However, long fights and fights of lethal outcome are on record. A bull elk that loses its footing during the fight is likely to be gored to death.

Usually, spike bulls do not see ferocious, bone-breaking combat such as larger bulls

*Estrus in elk is not showy. The receptive cow allows the bull to lick her vulva and place his chin on her croup while continuing to lick, a prelude to mounting. Pre-copulatory mounts test a cow's readiness to stand and also place the bull in a position for the dramatic copulatory thrust.*

occasionally deliver. Nevertheless, spike bulls do get wounded. They receive about thirty cuts and punctures per rutting season, but a few do better than that. One of the most-wounded elk I examined was a spike who had some seventy cuts and punctures.

As estrus approaches, the cow elk changes somewhat in her normal behavior. She licks her flank frequently, feeds less, stands for longer pauses between periods of feeding, and finds herself more and more often near the herd bull. She tolerates the courtship approach of the bull, who spends increasingly more time with her. The bull also licks the female extensively about the croup, back, withers, neck, head, and perianal region. When she rests and he steps up, she may stretch out on the ground. She may even suddenly attack other cows.

After a long bout of licking, the bull may put his neck over the cow's croup, the first sign that mounting is imminent. The first mounts are all preliminaries, but the real copulation is unmistakable, for the bull suddenly rears and jumps upward. His hind hooves leave the ground. The cow bounces forward and stops with spread legs and arched back. Soon she urinates, a good sign that she has been bred. The bull, as if suddenly "relieved," may furiously attack rivals in his vicinity.

This is, more or less, the normal course of events, provided the bull is still fresh and is experienced. When he is exhausted, or when he is a green youngster, the cow in heat may take over and court the bull. That can develop into quite a show. She may rub her body along his chest, butt him, lick his face, neck, and rear, and may try to mount him. She may rub her

*Female courtship is not common, but is rather showy when it does take place, particularly when the estrous female mounts the bull. A bull's failure to copulate may happen early in the rut with the first cow in heat, or when bulls are exhausted late in the rut, or when bulls are young and inexperienced.*

(Left) After the bulls have regained a little strength following the stresses of the rutting season, they join other bulls and begin to distance themselves from female company.

head in the urine-soaked earth of his rutting wallow, and then, head lowered in mock "antler threat," frolic before the bull. She clearly acts to excite the bull. Eventually it works and he is roused into breeding her. While the cow is in heat the bull checks attentively on her and may stop repeatedly to lick her on the head, neck and withers.

The first bulls to enter the rut are the old, big fellows. Where the rut is long, as in California, a group of cows may be herded by a succession of herd bulls. The exhausted bulls are replaced by fresh ones that were less successful earlier in the rut. The exhausted bulls start to recover from the strains and wounds of the rut by feeding and resting, preferably somewhere in hiding. By now they have lost nearly all of their body stores, they have many antler wounds to heal out, and they must recover some fat stores to face the long winter ahead. The drama of contests dies down as young bulls try their luck at finding cows in heat, while the old bulls move off and soon form male clubs away from female groups.

*(Left) Spike bulls, dislocated from nursery herds by big bulls during the rutting season, may wander off on their own into areas of unsuitable habitat. (Below) Mortality among spike bulls is significant.*

After the rut, spikes make it back to the cow groups. In large herds they may form subgroups of their own. Mortality among spike bulls in winter is significant; their weathered skulls are commonly found bleaching on mountain slopes. I have found them, not infrequently, when searching for bighorn sheep remains.

Are young bull elk particularly susceptible to die-offs? Apparently they are. This may be related to their wandering about and exploring. When elk are placed in large fenced enclosures from which they cannot stray, one finds a larger segment of bulls in the fenced populations than in wild, free-roaming populations.

After the great excitement of the rut, the continuity of the species is up to pregnant female elk. They must nurture the developing embryos in their wombs while the big bulls attempt simply to survive. Some reckless breeders and fighters do not succeed in that task—exhaustion, depletion of body stores, and infections from the many wounds they receive take their toll. The cycle of annual renewal will not return to the rutting behavior of the big bulls for another ten months or more. Until then the surviving bulls are on vacation, preparing themselves for the next big show ahead.

THROUGH THE SEASONS

*Like all grazers adapted to open landscapes and escaping predators by running, elk prefer flat, unobstructed footing and a clear view into the distance, as is found on the frozen surfaces of large lakes and rivers.*

The elk, despite its wide range and occupation of diverse habitats in North America, is essentially a creature of distinct seasons—of long winters with strong winds and low temperatures, of short but productive summers.

Existing in seasonal climates requires an ability to change with environmental conditions. For elk it means, besides constant vigilance to avoid predators, to be able to efficiently digest fresh, nutritious forage in one season, mature plants in another, dead plants in a third, and decaying one's in a fourth. An elk's rumen changes in size and internal micro-anatomy to accommodate these seasonal differences in food. Seasonal climates demand that one save nutrients and energy from the excesses of one season, summer, to the scarcity of another, winter. Opportunism is the hallmark of adaptability, however, and elk are opportunistic feeders that shift with good fortune.

Besides feeding, other elk activities wax and wane with the change of seasons. At least for bulls, reproduction is brief and seasonal. After the stresses and terror of the rut, they are on vacation for eleven months of the year. That does not apply to females, though, for they are either pregnant or lactating virtually year around.

The vagaries of winter mean elk must deal with snow in all its manifestations. They must endure howling blizzards as well as icing of the range when a cold snap follows warm chinook winds and freezes partially melted snow. Slick, water-covered ice on lakes in spring no longer makes frozen lakes good escape terrain. Thin ice on rivers in early winter and deep snowdrifts hinder elk, but not wolves. Ice floes grinding along rivers during break-up, plate ice piling up in large barriers along the shores, and snow

*A bull elk, apparently wounded and weakened by a mountain lion's attack, loses his struggle to cross a raging river. This occurred in March, when elk are still weakened by winter's stress.*

slides or even avalanches on grassy mountain slopes all create barriers to elk movement.

Elk must be able to find alternate forage when late winter and spring rains shower grasslands and lock the forage into sheets of hard ice. No elk can paw through ice to the grasses below. They must move into timber where the snow is still soft. Here they feed on dead forbs or browse. In ranch country, elk must also learn to avoid harm when they raid haystacks, as ranchers quickly lose their humor over elk piracy.

In his younger years as an elk control officer in southwestern Alberta, my friend Andy Russell spent many a freezing moonlit night protecting haystacks from elk. Those elk had learned a thing or two about ranchers, but also about bright and dark nights, and about the essence of safety, which to them was to return well before dawn to the protection of Waterton Lakes National Park.

Here, these animals, so quick to avoid humans on ranched land, flouted about in full view of visitors, utterly confident that they were safe.

Elk are good learners. In Banff National Park during the 1950s and 1960s, elk numbers were reduced annually by shooting. The goal was less to maintain productive populations than to protect the park's vegetation from overgrazing. The park elk soon learned to keep clear off men, particularly uniformed men in small green trucks. Big elk herds would clump well away from shore on the frozen surface of the Vermilion Lakes near Banff. Tourist car after tourist car could drive by without stirring the mass of elk, but if a warden's green pickup truck rolled by, a wave of motion went through the herd. If the truck slowed, the herd began to move. If the truck stopped, the elk ran off the

*(Left) When sun or wind glazes or packs snow into impenetrable sheets on open meadows, elk move into the shadows and stillness of dense forests where the snow remains soft.*

*(Below) Debilitated, exhausted, ill and inattentive, this bull is about to succumb to the stresses of the rut, wounding, and the drain of low temperatures and difficult, meager foraging. The next day only a few scavenged bones, scattered hair and red snow attest to his existence.*

ice, crossed the railway, and went off into the timber beyond.

Are elk naturally spooked by humans? Try telling that today to one of the residents of Banff who can't get a past a nasty six-point bull on his lawn, or to the golf player picking his way through a resting herd on the elk-manured greens below the craggs of the Banff Springs Hotel, or the tourists just chased off the trail by a tooth-grinding, wicked mommy elk. Was there ever a time when these humorless thugs were spooky? Indeed there was, and still is — outside the park where they are hunted. Elk control was terminated in Canadian national parks in the late 1960s when second thoughts about such interference with nature became audible, as had predator control a little earlier. However, while control operations lasted, efficient teams of wardens gunning for elk soon

left their mark—spooky elk and squabbling ravens over steaming gut piles in the snow.

Learning, at which elk are so very good, is an inherent part of adapting to sharply differing seasons. Relative brain size increases in mammals from the equator to the poles, which is seen nowhere better than in our own evolution. We went from small-brained tropical forest apes, before the Ice Ages, to large-brained super-carnivores in late glacial periods. Brain size also appears to increase with diversity of skills mastered. Life in "one season" in the tropics requires specialization, a narrow but highly efficient adaptation. Life in four seasons requires a diversity of adaptations.

The progression of the seasons sees elk moving between areas that offer distinctive short-term advantages. This is most conspicuous in the

*(Left) For bulls, who need to grow large bodies and antlers, the availability of large amounts of high-quality forage in summer is crucial. (Below) Malformed antlers usually result from damage to growing, velvet antlers, such as probably happened to the bull on the left, but asymmetries also arise due to injuries of the body, and probably due to excessive toxicity of summer forage.*

mountains. Here elk show predictable migrations from low, restricted winter ranges—where they may have to be maintained by supplemental feeding as is widely and successfully done in Wyoming—to big, productive subalpine summer ranges. Given tall mountains, elk follow sprouting, highly nutritious vegetation up the south slopes as "spring" progresses in elevation, and down the north slopes in late summer.

As able opportunists, elk move to the best forage wherever they find it, and forage is rarely better than on areas where climax forests were devastated a few years prior by raging wildfires. The heat kills off the trees and encourages suckering from root bowls of willows, aspen, cottonwoods or birches. A plethora of wildflowers, grasses and sedges sprout from the soil now fertilized by ashes. The multitude of suckers is almost free of toxins, quite contrary to the situation when only one sucker is trying to reach for the sparse light in a dusky forest. Such lone suckers are very toxic. The foliage in "burns" is exceptionally nutritious as it bathes in sunlight and fertility. Deer, moose and elk flocking to the burns soon show off with larger antlers, higher birth rates, big bodies and much improved survival. Thus, thunderstorms and lightning are friends of deer, moose, elk or deer mice, but by burning old-growth forests they are enemies of woodland caribou, tree lichen and snowshoe hares. Where one wins, another loses. The bonanza does not last on the burns as they grow old, for woody shrubs and trees soon proliferate, choking off light and nutrition to forbs, sedges, grasses and low shrubs. Trees from the climax community invade the burns

*When an elk loses its antlers, it loses its identity and rank. At once it is challenged by others and must fight for status, but now with the aid of its front legs rather than its antlers.*

*Occasionally a bull with budding antlers forgets the loss of its hard antlers and threatens another with his lowered head. This threat is, nevertheless, clearly understood by subordinates.*

THROUGH THE SEASONS                    135

and grow vigorously. After several decades the burn is no more, its seral communities replaced by young climax forests that exclude elk, except to grant them shelter and security.

Seasonal changes also affect elk nutrition and antler growth. The availability of high-quality forage in late summer is especially important for maximum antler growth. Lowland elk bulls, faced by fibrous and toxic late summer vegetation, may suffer shortages of nutrition for antler growth and, consequently, grow shorter, straighter and lighter antlers than do mountain bulls. Antlers are very sensitive to the quality and quantity of food as well as its time of availability. As heavily grazed plants grow toxic to protect themselves, elk are ever more burdened by the noxious chemical loads they must metabolize away, and that leaves relatively less available energy for body and antler growth.

I suspect that high toxicity might also affect the sensitive growth of the antlers, resulting in asymmetrical racks. In productive lowlands, highly nutritious spring growth may be so rich that elk grow quickly on that forage and, as a result, have exceptionally big bodies, strong bones, and thick-beamed antlers. But that happy state of affairs does not last. Soon the plants grow fibrous and toxic, and though there may be lots of "green," there is little good forage. The intense productivity pulse of fertile lowlands, followed by a rapid decline in forage quality, may thus translate into large-bodied bulls that carry thick-beamed, but light, straight, short-tined antlers. That is an example of "ecotypic" growth, however, not subspecific characteristics.

Groups of wintering bulls begin to break up when the animals start shedding their antlers in late March. Antlers represent the "personality"

*In later summer, after some 150-170 days of antler growth, the nourishing velvet dries and is stripped off the newly formed bone. Velvet shedding may be completed within a day. The light-colored antlers soon darken as residual blood on their surface is combined with stains from plant juices in the bark of shrubs and trees horned by the bull.*

THROUGH THE SEASONS        137

of a bull, the means by which he is recognized by other bulls. The antler drop causes lack of recognition and consequent aggression between antlerless bulls and those still retaining their headgear. This breaks up the fraternal groups that had moved about and sparred together so amiably before. Now the antlerless bulls cannot prevail against those with antlers. So, having lost status, they move on.

Unlike mule and white-tailed deer, bull elk retain their antlers until spring, and they need to. As long as the bulls retain their antlers, there is relative peace within the group of wintering bulls. Strife costs energy, and energy needs to be conserved in winter. Thus in red deer species, the longer the winter, the longer the bulls retain their antlers. Consequently, the cold-adapted elk, with a long history in Ice Age Siberia, retains its antlers much longer than does the warm-adapted red deer of Europe. That has consequences: Red deer shed their antlers early but regrow them in 150-170 days, as do elk. However, red deer males, after shedding, stand about with cleaned-off antlers for six to eight weeks before the rut. They enjoy a lazy existence between shedding velvet and rutting. The bull elk does not. It ruts right after shedding velvet. It may even begin rutting with its antler velvet incompletely shed.

Here nature plays a trick on elk in California. The bulls there have remained "programmed" as ever by the long Siberian winter they no longer experience in the balmy south. However, the cows have not. The essence of security for calf elk is to minimize, through spacing, the chance of meeting a predator. The spacing may exist in a corporeal sense — cow elk about to give birth do

*Shedding and regrowing the hair coat in spring is a heavy physiological burden carried out at the expense of other body tissues. That burden is eased only by the availability of rich forage and mineral licks.*

leave other elk and seek isolation and seclusion. However, the spacing may also be in time. That is, it is advantageous — within limits — for the cow elk to give birth at a time different from others in her herd. If this temporally spaced calving truly proves advantageous to a given population, natural selection would quickly favor cows that give birth earlier or later than the norm. That also means, of course, favoring cows that come into heat later or earlier than the norm. Consequently, the calving and the breeding season would begin to stretch ever longer, as long as permitted by the availability of food in spring at calving. This has been the case in California elk, where some cows begin to become receptive and force the bulls, still in velvet-covered antlers, to begin bugling, rutting and fighting. This is another phenomenon testifying to the fact that elk are rather recent immigrants to the warm climates of North America.

Seasonal change accounts for the lush vegetation of spring and summer. Yet, for all the greenery that we see, not very much of it translates into elk muscle, sinew, fat and bone. Not only is the nutrient value of much of that greenery too low, or the cellulose fibers too thick and abundant for the elk's microflora rumen to digest efficiently, but some of the plants are much too toxic as well. These toxins are costly to metabolize away or they interfere with the fermentation process in the rumen, robbing the elk of important nutrients. So, elk must search for the most nutritious and least toxic plants.

Plant food has low digestibility, even though elk, as ruminants, digest forage more efficiently than do, for instance, horses. From 100 units of good food, elk can digest about 45 units. Of those 45 units of energy, roughly 25 are lost as heat in the process of being digested, the rest is

*Elk are rather lazy — and need to be. Under the best of forage conditions their intake barely exceeds the demands of their metabolism.*

THROUGH THE SEASONS   139

converted to body tissue or to work. Thus, the elk's caloric performance is at best 25 percent efficient, or, for elk, the cost of living is high. Even in summer the difference between the daily cost of living and the intake is not great. In winter it is a negative balance. So, do not be surprised if elk appear relatively lazy, if they play only rarely and then primarily in late spring, for they cannot afford to squander energy. However, our notions of energy matter little. What does count is there be energy available when needed to supplement poor quality winter food, or augment the high cost of healing a wounded body after the rut, or help push up the antlers in spring before the greenery gets lush, or help grow the elk baby, or to aid in the production of milk in those crucial weeks after birth.

Granted this high cost to stay alive, and a dependence on stored fat to cover the shortfalls,

any harassment of elk by humans is added cost to an already costly existence. That cost is always passed on to the unborn calf. When there is a big deficit in cost over income, it is reproduction that suffers. After all, each elk at birth must be of a given minimum weight to survive the first day of life. At birth, calf weights range from 19 to 45 pounds; optimum birth weights, however, are from 30 to 40 pounds. Elk calves too small at birth may be too weak to even rise and suckle; small calves, if not lost, may grow into runts that cannot survive winter. To ensure minimum survivable size at birth, elk calves need a good supply of nutrients and energy. Consequently, to maximize reproduction, elk cows need freedom from unnecessary disturbance during winter. Coping with cougars and wolves is bad enough without adding joy-riding snowmobilers, four-wheel drivers and other forms of human disturbance

*A newborn calf, cleaned by its mother of birth membranes and amniotic fluid, looks into a bright new world. The cow also cleans the birth site, removing all olfactory evidence of the calf's presence, to minimize attracting predators.*

THROUGH THE SEASONS          141

to the stress level. If elk are disturbed too much in an area and find night grazing there also insufficient, they vacate it for a more quiet existence. That can amount to a loss of habitat, which comes at a very high cost to elk.

In spring and summer when elk are renewing their bodies, growing antlers and a hair coat, producing milk and laying down stores of fat, vitamins, and minerals for future use, mineral licks become very important. Growing a thick, long coat is a very costly exercise in terms of energy and rare nutrients. There is competition among different organs for those nutrients. Cows that are lactating, for instance, put the precious nutrients first into milk and then into a hair coat. Consequently, cows are last to shed the old coat and regrow the new.

Inorganic sulfur is one of the essential rare nutrients in mineral licks, for inorganic sulfur is incorporated in the elk's rumen by the microflora into its own tissue. The microflora use the inorganic sulphur in synthesizing the vital amino acids systein and methionine. Elk, in turn, digest the bacteria and protozoa supplied with these protein building blocks so very important in growing hair, horn and connective tissue. Mineral licks are important, too, for sodium, and also for magnesium salts that are an important aid in the orderly digestion of fresh spring flora. This obviously explains why elk visit mineral licks when they are growing new hair and antlers, producing milk, and restoring the body for the mating season ahead.

In spring, as well as visiting mineral licks, elk move to calving grounds that offer some security to the widely distributed cows. Grizzly and black bears, wolves, wolverine and coyotes will try hard to locate the tasty newborns. Even eagles

*A bull elk licks dead trees in a thermal area. Not everything elk do is understandable to us, as yet. Does this bull lick minerals wicked up and left as evaporites? Non-forage sources of minerals are very important to elk; they may even chew bones they find on the range.*

*Seclusion and cleanliness mean safety. Her calf, hidden on a small island, the cow sucks up the calf's feces and urine and cleans off its anal area. Unlike human children, calf elk appear to enjoy having their ears washed. The cow thoroughly licks the calf before allowing it to hide once again.*

may strike elk calves, as one golden eagle did right in front of me on a day-old calf. He wheeled in to hit it four times and made it cry and stagger with each blow, but did not break the calf's skin. The aggressive raptor abandoned the calf when he saw me coming. The little elk then crouched and lay stiff as a board at my feet. A group of bighorn ewes came along and examined it cautiously. When the sheep left, I departed too, in the hope that its mommy found the little elk.

Calf elk, in addition to their spotted coats for camouflage, are nearly devoid of scent. After calving, the cow elk removes all the afterbirth, eats the birth-fluid-soaked earth, and licks clean the birth site. That's a good way to reduce advertising to the sensitive noses of bears and wolves that a calf elk was born.

The newborn calf hides itself masterfully and is suckled just four to six times a day to maximize the time it spends in the safety of hiding. Consequently, the duration of suckling in elk is long compared with, for instance, caribou. (A caribou calf follows its mother virtually at all times.) During suckling visits the cow elk removes the calf's urine and feces, and she licks the calf extensively. Cleanliness is safety to the calf.

Sound signals also mean safety. Calves may bleat when in danger, and a cow elk readily rushes in to protect her calf against minor predators such as coyotes. These little wild dogs succeed only too well in the absence of the cow. Small calves drop into hiding upon the alarm bark of the cow elk; they come out of hiding or bleat in response to a high-pitched nasal whine uttered by the cow.

*Calves form groups of playmates, away from their mothers but never far removed. They practice adult behaviors very early, particularly how to dominate others and how to court and breed.*

**THROUGH THE SEASONS**     145

When the calves grow larger, however, they will run to the cow during an alarm, ready to flee with her.

The calves, after a week in hiding, join into noisy, playful nursery groups as the summer herd forms again. One can then hear the calls of cows and calves a long way on a summer day in the mountains. Now on the summer range, the bulls will join the cows and calves again in late August. The bulls begin to call now, ever so often, and, with their freshly cleaned antlers, begin sparring with one anther. The rut is soon to begin. After its passage, the calves will continue to live in the female herds. The bulls will pull out to winter on their own.

*A yearling female is chased off by its mother, who already has given birth to another calf. Only if the newborn dies may the cow re-adopt her yearling, but even then the bond weakens as the young elk becomes increasingly independent.*

With the arrival of spring the yearling elk suffers a painful separation from its mother. This happens about two weeks before the yearling's new brother or sister is about to be born and the cows again segregate from the other elk. During the separation, the yearlings follow barren cows or roam about on their own. They rejoin the nursery herds after the new calves emerge with their dams. Some yearlings find their mother minus a brother or sister and are reunited for another year of mothering. However, the yearling bulls will find their pleasant summer cruelly terminated when the big bulls return for the rut, while the highly developed female yearlings, on rare occasions, become sexually mature and objects of attention of the big bulls. Most of the young female elk, though, will remain barren in their second year of life, be bred short of two and a half years of age, and give birth at three. According to these rituals, elk life is renewed year after year, and so we hope, elk may carry on forever young.

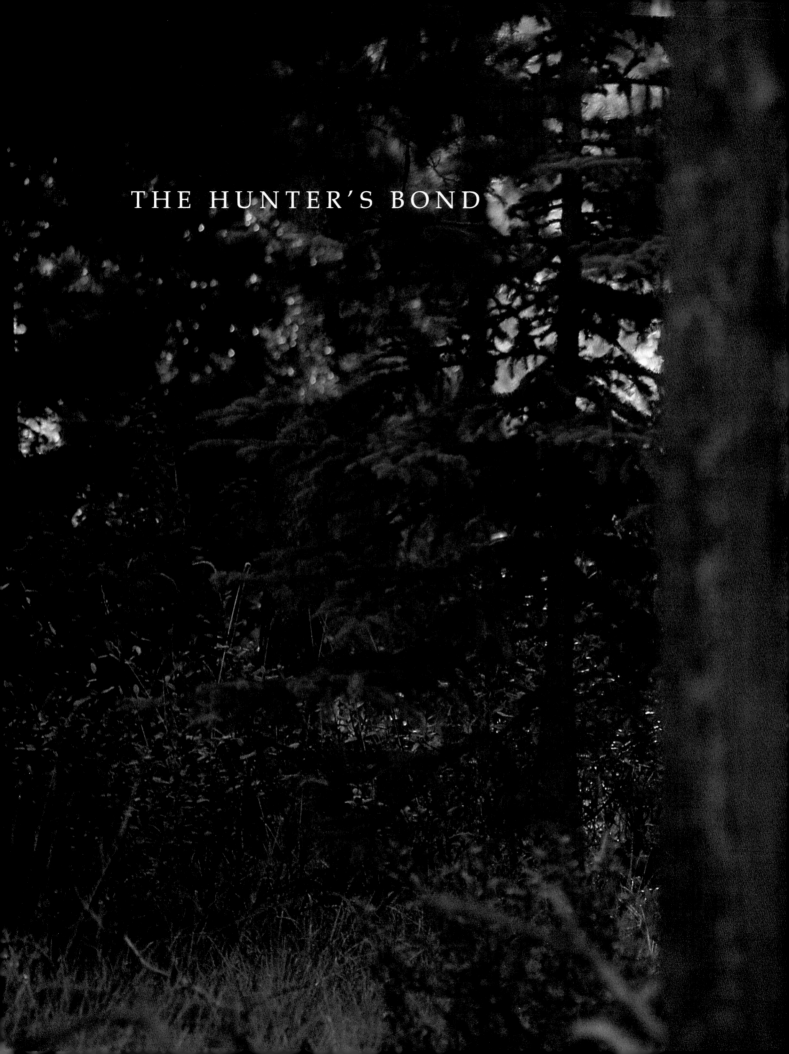

THE HUNTER'S BOND

*Big bulls, symmetrical antlers and lush green meadows*
*are linked in a chain of cause and effect.*

*Elk live well where land and water meet.*

There is a bond between elk and us, the ancient bond of the predator to its prey. That such a bond exists should not be surprising—the elk and his relatives have been a source of sustenance to humans in their long period as fellow travelers over the same land. Well over a quarter of a million years ago, people of our parent species, *Homo erectus,* ate red deer around hearths in a warm inter-glacial Europe and used its antlers as raw materials for tools. We don't know how these early people hunted the big deer. Their abundant tools, their food remains and evidence of their camp activities, preserved in the travertine of calcium-rich springs, suggest the working of red deer skins with flint tools, and that the antlers of big red deer were shaped into clubs or digging tools.

While elk and red deer never assumed the prominence of reindeer in the archeological sites of people of the Upper Paleolithic, our direct ancestors, they rank along with bison, horses and mammoths as important prey. This is most evident during warmer phases of the last major glaciation, when reindeer remains became distinctly less common in the bone middens of ancient camps, while those of red deer, ibex, chamois, and of wild cattle, ancestors of domestic cattle, increased in frequency.

We have been carnivores a very long time, and our infatuation with prey species may be more biological than we care to admit. Of course, we don't care to admit that we do things irrationally, for ancient, adaptive reasons. Heaven help us—we are above that sort of thing. Why, we are cultured! Still, we groom ourselves as do all primates; culture only obfuscates the matter (and allows vendors of

*Excitement works both ways — for us when sighting a bull close up, and for the bull sighting us. This bull shows it by opening wide the preorbital gland just ahead of his eye.*

THE HUNTER'S BOND          151

toilet articles to make a killing). We show off to others in subtle and not so subtle dominance games—as do all large mammals, but we sophisticate such showing off and call it "culture." Like other animals, we also fall prey to sexual releasers (sometimes served up in erotic magazines). We create "cave" after "cave" and spend over 90 percent of our time in their cozy security, more than our cavemen ancestors ever could. We light up the night using every feeble excuse to do it.

This is not the place to argue about a view of man that sends waves of anger through the liberal arts community. However, scientists who study animal societies think that a pretty fair case can be made for the view that we almost compulsively satisfy by cultural means our deepest biological drives. And so it would appear that our old prey still excites us, still sends shivers down our spines. Let an elk step out along a national park road and watch a traffic jam of cars develop. People crowd in to see, to gesticulate, to laugh and to photograph—all terribly excited.

Does hunting have deep, instinctive roots? It can grip emotions as powerfully as reproduction. Hunting our old prey can be as gripping, as biologically fulfilling, as any human activity. When the hunt overtakes our very being, when old men are rejuvenated, when the urge to possess, to have this prey corrupts men, then it becomes hard to believe that hunting is an acquired cultural activity without deeper roots. It is thrilling to see, to film, to photograph, but to hunt and kill an elk can be overwhelming. Whatever its roots, hunting is so powerful that it may carry off

reason as its slave, but it can also bond the most unlikely of people to a common cause. Hunting forges concern and action for wildlife conservation, for the hunter's affection for the quarry runs deep.

Moving as it is to stand on a paved highway in a national park, only feet away from a bugling bull elk herding his harem and challenging rivals, it is more moving still to "become a bull elk" when hunting. "In hunting, the hunter must become the hunted," so Douglas Cardinal, a Cree shaman and distinguished Canadian architect, related to me. To hunt your prey you must become one with it—you must think and act like your quarry or it detects you as a fraud, and in the old days, at least, you and your family went hungry.

Is that the root of our superlative, in fact uniquely human abilities to mimic animal sounds and act out convincing pantomimes?

While scientific observation of free-living elk exposes much of their lives, so does the hunt. To play a bull in rut convincingly requires much more than being able to imitate the long-stretched vocalizations of the bull elk with a hand-held elk bugle. When a hunter blows an elk bugle, he blows it to sound like a bull elk. Because of nuances in each hunter's calling, however, he develops a vocal signature, much as have individual bull elk in their own calls. By listening to other elk, a bull can trace the movements of rivals in space, and because of that, it has expectations about how rivals are likely to move. Consequently, it can intercept or avoid rivals with precision, even though it only hears their voice.

*(Left) Only very confident bulls horn trees when challenging others. (Below) To be convincing when playing elk, one must not only imitate the bugle of a bull but modulate the call according to different conditions. Bulls searching for cows, bulls with cows, and bulls herding cows all sound different.*

In addition to their vocalizations, elk also make sounds with their antlers when challenging rivals. To an elk hunter, then, a piece of antler is a good accompaniment to a man-made elk bugle. However, only confident bulls thrash trees with their antlers. Confident bulls not only scream at the top of their voice, but also spray urine copiously. This is done with powerful contractions of the belly muscles and thus affects the diaphragm, and colors the manner of bugling.

Then there is the hunter's strategy. A really big bull with a harem is not keen for contest, but can be so motivated if enough cows begin to show an interest in the "voice" of the approaching stranger. Then the harem bull's herding increases, and with that his bugling at cows. Otherwise, it is bulls of the second order of size and power that answer the bugle and move in to take a look at the new "elk" on the block. Now the hunter must act the part of the bull elk, preferably the part of a challenger without a harem. Such a bull moves in rapidly on any harem herder. And that's what a bull with a harem expects. He will not come to the bugle, he expects the bugler to move in. He may then grow silent and herd off his harem. A single bull, however, is likely to accept the challenge if it is convincing. He will answer—after a pause—and expects an answer—also after a pause. If he has nothing else to do, he may come, but will halt periodically to vigorously horn a small pine or spruce tree. If you fail to horn back, you are classified as a coward, and the bull may lose

*(Top left) In undisturbed elk populations, the audible clashes of antlers are heard day and night as part of the normal rutting season. (Bottom left) Bulls looking for action are attracted not only by bugles but also by noises such as breaking branches that may indicate the movement of a herd or a rival.*

interest. He may answer, but he will never come to your bugle again because he recognizes your vocal signature. However, you can still move in on such a bull, as he may still answer you but not take you seriously any longer. Once a coward, always a coward.

In short, bull elk learn about rivals and also learn about odd, peculiar calls and puzzling behavior of human callers—and once they have associated such with human scent they become very cautious about any bugling sound. Would you expect anything else from an intelligent animal?

Yet there is hardly a concert more moving than that of a gathering of bulls in a moonlit mountain valley where the echo reverberates their calls and the clash of antlers rings through the darkness. This is raw, primeval nature. So are the groans of bulls at night when they hear a hunter's footsteps on the trail as he moves up to meet the dawn on a mountain ridge. The bull's deep-chested challenge is to test who goes there. We cannot reply to it, not with our puny chests nor with current technology. And it is raw nature indeed when a bull rushes in on the purported rival, screaming in apparent rage, splintering saplings with his antlers—and yet it's all bluff. Let him twig to the fact that a human, not a rival, is before him and the bull vanishes silently, and better informed as well. Yet a hunter can on occasion play the game so well that a bull rushing off at the sight of the hunter can be induced to spin around and come back for another look by the hunter's powerful bugle. A convincing bugling performance can be

*When rushing a rival, an aggressive bull curls up his lips, exposing his short, blunt canines. For the elk's distant ancestors, these teeth, then much larger, were formidable weapons.*

*A bull elk under an early morning rainbow*
*formed by a steaming meadow.*

thrilling, such as when cow elk become nosy and walk in to investigate the perceived bull, but it can also be dangerous: I gave up after being stalked by three hunters.

However, elk are fair game not only during the rut, but also late in fall when snow covers the ground, the air is chilled, and sun-dogs glow in the sky. Tracking an elk through a snow-clad forest requires one to forget all thoughts of comfort, to test the wind, to listen and cautiously circle ahead, to move as silently as possible. Where elk are much hunted, this is not a fruitful way to hunt because the ever-alert elk soon detect and correctly interpret the approaching hunter. However, where elk and hunters rarely meet and elk are less wary, this is a fine way to approach elk.

Nor must it be a big bull that we take. Ideally, hunting should cull the expendable, and most of the elk taken should be calves, not adults. A calf is the elk least tested by nature. It is the most likely to succumb to winter stresses and predation and can be removed with no damage to the population. That's not true of removing full-grown though still-young bulls, or of cows, young ones in particular. The old trappers had the right idea when elk were abundant: Kill a calf for food. It is much better meat than that of a big bull, anyway. When there is a choice, taking a calf and forgoing the big bull takes discipline and the courage to withstand uninformed peer-pressure, particularly today when the macho killing of big bulls is celebrated in sporting journals.

Other cultures than our own have hunted elk, but in different ways and usually with the purpose of taking only the largest bulls. The hunting of elk, or, more appropriately red deer—"noble" deer as Europeans call them—is deeply rooted in Old World custom. The hunting of red deer was a glorious event in medieval times, when great hunts were held by nobility, hunts notable and expensive enough to diminish the treasuries of noblemen and kings. Large antlers were exchanged as princely gifts. Stags were featured in paintings, engraved on weapons and sculptured into statues. Stags with mythical powers were featured in religious tales, such as the conversion of St. Hubert, the patron saint of huntsmen. He, a bishop, but also a daring, ruthless hunter, was converted when a crucifix appeared to him between the antlers of a stag. That was in 683 AD, in the Ardennes Forest of Frey, in southern Belgium. St. Hubert's day, November 3, is celebrated to this day.

European nobility, but also its all-too-worldly clergy, were infatuated with red deer. No peasant was permitted to fence his meager fields and orchards to prevent deer from raiding the crops. He had to watch, impotent to act, as deer devoured the meager fruits of his hard labor. Woe to the serf caught chasing the deer away, or worse yet, inflicting bodily harm on them! Unspeakably cruel punishment was meted out to him, often instantly, by the foresters protecting the "noble" deer. Those that dared kill the deer were often executed with severe torture, had their property seized, and their families sold into slavery. The higher clergy of the day was at times even more vicious than the nobility in protecting deer. The 17th century Archbishop of Salzburg, Michael von Khinburg, had a man executed in the market place by having him sown in a deer skin and torn to pieces by dogs. He personally blew

the hunting horn to start the public spectacle. What was the condemned man's crime? He had found a stag who had died from wounds inflicted in a hunt on his land, and had cut up the animal for his use. Some clergy, however, like Martin Luther, did rail against the draconian practices of the day.

Not only had the serf to look upon deer marauding his fields, or shake in fear of being caught being disloyal to his lord, but he had to perform unpaid labor in fostering the great hunts. Roedel, a famous German wildlife photographer, records in his book on red deer that the hunting parties of Philip of Hessia (1518-1567) contained 100-200 horses. Each hunt required three relays of horses and hounds, for a stag could run for hours before coming to bay. Thus hundreds of horses galloped for hours across the land, much to the anguish of the helpless peasants. And that could be repeated 40 times a season, or more.

As to size, the largest antlers of the medieval red deer significantly exceeded in mass the largest antlers of current record bull elk in North America. These monstrosities can still be examined, for instance, in the Moritz Burg near Dresden in Germany. The largest set of antlers, after centuries of drying, weighs 43.7 pounds (19.865 kg) with a small skull cap. The largest elk antlers, including the upper skull, that I ever saw weighed only 37 pounds (17.5 kg). In body size, large medieval stags were as large as the largest of our bull elk. We know, because the medieval nobility was obsessed with weighing the big stags they killed.

The huge antlers and bodies of medieval red deer stage were a willful result of highly skilled

management by foresters in the service of nobility. These were "man-made" deer, in the best sense of the word. Stags were managed deliberately for large size because of state prestige, and the foresters had to deliver, like it or not. And deliver they did. Forests in those days were managed less for wood than for "mast," the crops of acorns and beechnuts. Mast was vitally important for raising hogs. Without mast there were no hams, no sausage, no bacon, and above all, no precious lard. So, medieval forests were made up of old, well-spaced trees that let plenty of light fall on the floor, encouraging a rich ground flora. The rich natural feed did foster large deer, but the foresters also saw to it that the deer got the best the land could grow: the crops in the fields, gardens and orchards tended by the peasants. Crops were a superior feed and they also concentrated the deer, allowing foresters to predict the whereabouts of the largest stags when the time for hunting came at the lord's behest.

Not all red deer hunts before the hounds were of short duration. Some deer were chased five hours or more. The record was set by a stag, a mediocre ten-pointer at that, which lasted through a ten-hour chase followed by 40 dogs and the hunting party of Count Wilhelm Friedrich of Brandenburg. In the 18th century, a stag hunted by the Count of Anhalt Dessau ran ten Prussian miles (over 74 km or 46.4 imperial miles). The count killed eight horses trying to ride that stag to bay. Some count, some stag!

When domestic horses came to North America in the 16th century, native people became some of the finest horsemen ever, but there is little in the historical record to indicate their running elk on horseback. Horses were used to run buffalo, but running elk was considered by natives inefficient and dangerous. Single elk were recognized as swift runners, and bull elk were known to turn on horse and rider. There was, after all, no pack of hounds to distract a bull elk, as was the case for stags in Europe. There is some conflicting information about California elk, as the Old Spanish Californians, so Theodore van Dyke recounts, found it easy to run down and rope them—unless the elk ran into the quagmire of the tule marshes. Teddy Roosevelt found it very difficult to catch up on foot to walking elk. At a trot, he claims, wapiti progress very rapidly, particularly in broken terrain, and only a very good pony could catch up. Clearly, once startled, wapiti ran long distances. Roosevelt found wapiti to be fast runners, faster than mule deer, though not very enduring. A yearling elk may run flat out a few miles, but old, heavy bulls tired easily. Before the end of the 19th century, Roosevelt goes on to tell, when elk were still found on open prairie away from badlands and cover, they were run on occasion with horses, with and without the aid of hounds.

Native Americans did not greatly value the meat of elk, though they valued the hide. Elk were not much hunted as long as buffalo were abundant, but some hunting from horseback did occur. Apparently, when a herd of elk was surrounded and chased, the elk were slowed and exhausted by bumping into one another, apparently injuring individuals. Some would drop out and were killed by the hunters. This reflects in good part the speed and endurance of elk, their aggressive turning to fight pursuers, but also on their skillful use of cover, steep slopes and broken terrain where horsemen, and presumably other predators, hated to follow. Also, hunted wapiti learn fast and may choose broken terrain and cover where they hide, even crouch in cover, like white-tailed deer, while the bulls practice a silent rut.

How good is elk meat? Indian people, as discussed earlier, did not like it particularly and preferred moose or bison. It escapes me why this was the case. (Perhaps it was because elk meat, unlike the meat of bison, spoils easily in drying.) Teddy Roosevelt, in his days as a Montana rancher in the 1880s, preferred elk meat to that of mule deer. However, mule deer in sage-covered prairie can be occasionally less than delectable, as I can attest. The old Californians preferred the meat of their wild cattle to that of the then abundant elk. The meat of red deer is liked well enough in Europe to support a deer farming industry there and in New Zealand. However, for gourmet cooking, according to the great Escofier, only the meat of young animals is to be taken, while that of large stags is to be avoided. The meat of well-run red deer is, in fact, somewhat toxic, and thus hardly suitable for human consumption, even though running red deer with horse and hound was common in past centuries.

Chemically, the meat of wild elk and red deer, like that of other wild creatures, is rich in vitamins and minerals, compared to that of domestic livestock, and has less fat between the muscles. It is a truly natural product, unadulterated by manipulation such as injected antibiotics, growth hormones or vaccines. It is tasty enough, but it can be tough, and as raw material it is only as good as the cook handling it.

The elk roast in a hunter's house, however, is more than meat. It is a symbol and treated as such, no matter how it tastes. The meat of an elk from the mountains is a part of the mountains. It is a product of virgin wilderness soils, crystal clear waters, the flowers, grasses and trees that grow there, and the rain and snow that falls. We are what we eat, and by eating the elk we become, in a very literal sense, a part of those wild, clean mountains.

Yes, I'd rather you ate elk meat taken from the wild forests with skill, toil, and sweat. It keeps one honest in our culture of fancy illusions. For although we have stepped on the moon and shot our probes beyond the planets, we remain children of a fragile Earth, as much as the elk. The elk's meat reminds us where all our sustenance comes from—not from the supermarket counter, no matter how fancy the package, but from the biosphere that creates the miracle of life on our wonderful but ailing planet. The elk's meat is a bond that unites us, prey and hunter, to the great circle of life and death about us. An elk's warm heart in one's hand reminds us of the eternal tragedy of our life, that to eat we must kill, that we only live through the life of other beings. Whether we eat elk stew or granola bars, the fact stands that both are products of life, be it animal or plant. All our food was once vibrant, throbbing life. Crunch a salad and your teeth shear through living protoplasm. Crunch granola and you crush a multitude of broken and roasted bodies of plant children, sweetened with the life-sustaining essence that bees collected for their brood. We live by eating life.

Hunting elk or deer, if insisted upon by many citizens, translates into political will to keep the mountains and forests wild and free. Take away the right of citizens to gain elk or deer by legal means, as occurred in medieval times, and elk and deer slip into the control again of a few with power, to be enjoyed and often despoiled by them for frivolous pleasures. Ironically, the multitudes that care for wildlife but receive very limited material gain from it have proven the best protectors of their prey and its habitat. Surprisingly, this foundation of successful conservation of wildlife and nature, *allocation by law*, is also the foundation of wildlife management in native societies here and abroad. But maybe that is not that surprising after all.

Protect elk and their habitat and along with elk and deer can dwell cougars, coyote and bear, all nature's agents. Here there is room for all the "weeds" and "vermin" that on cultivated land is not, and often cannot be tolerated. The wilderness is not only nature's painting, as some would treat it, but the original basis of our existence, and the guarantee of a future. And that is what the elk roast at Thanksgiving ultimately represents.

THE FUTURE

I wish I could be cheerful about the elk's future. Alas, I cannot. I will lead you now, briefly, through the insidious problems facing this magnificent creature.

Along with existing problems wildlife face with widespread loss of habitat, and with global pollution by deadly chemicals that strangle their reproduction, there is also an international market that pays premium prices for their carcasses, alive and dead.

We face today in North America a deep, but still silent, crisis in wildlife conservation: the commercialization of wildlife. This crisis has grown, cancer-like, and its severity has not been sufficiently recognized or appreciated. The crisis is a determined effort to convert wildlife from a public to a private resource. Such a transfer is devastating to wildlife, including our elk.

There are and have been landowners, here and abroad, under whose loving care wildlife have found their only home, and who have greatly contributed to conservation. These landowners have remained incorruptible, but a corrupting force is afoot: money. There is money to be made from dead elk, a lot of money. However, to achieve maximum profits on elk in the international luxury market, one must first dismantle the policies and laws that have so successfully conserved wildlife for the last 75 years on this continent.

There are four basic North American conservation policies: (1) retain wildlife as a public resource, ensuring that nobody maintains large numbers of native wildlife for private manipulation and exploitation; (2) prohibit the sale of dead wildlife, except

furs; (3) allocate surplus wildlife by law to all citizens and avoid allocation by the pocketbook and special status, and (4) prohibit frivolous killing of wildlife.

If you want to make money from elk, you must have the ability to manipulate elk genetically, to exploit the whims of the market. Therefore, you must own elk to control them. To make money from elk you must be able to sell their parts—venison, velvet antlers, penises, tails and other parts—to the highest bidder. And with that you create an "infrastructure" of producers, processors, wholesale dealers and retailers, an ideal situation for laundering illegally killed public elk in the market. A legal market in dead wildlife may then be fed dead public wildlife by the clever and corrupt.

Allocating elk according to the power of the pocketbook excludes the very persons that future conservation depends on, young hunters, and passes elk on strictly to the highest bidders on private hunting ranches. However, those bidders want "quality" for their money. They may especially want "big antlers." Unscrupulous hunting ranch operators have been known to go to extremes, illegal or otherwise dangerous extremes such as genetic manipulation, to provide those so-called trophies.

To service market demands, hybridizing and breeding elk for "improved" characteristics are unavoidable for the elk industry. That means the destruction of adaptations of captive elk is also unavoidable. Also, to develop an industry in elk and other deer, be it for venison ranching or for sport hunting on private ranches, the animals need to be transported between jurisdictions.

Transporting elk between game breeders and sport ranches and other dealers in game animals means that elk will have to be free of diseases or they may infect other elk herds or livestock. In the process of shipping elk there are untold opportunities for diseases to transfer as the badly stressed, weakened elk meet other elk, deer, exotic game animals and livestock in quarantine stations, in auction halls, in transit, and on ranches. These are ideal situations for transferring diseases, particularly because many diseases cannot be diagnosed in living elk and because quarantine regulations are inadequate to detect the afflictions. In addition, there is a criminal element which not only illegally catches public elk for private gain, or engages in organized killing of public wildlife for profit, but also defies veterinary regulations. The latter guarantees that wild animals laden with diseases are transported, and so spread the diseases.

All this is current reality in the game ranching industry. In my home province of Alberta, for example, there are now about 4,000 elk behind game farm fences, but 150,000 are expected in a few years. Sixty-two game farms are currently under quarantine because of tuberculosis, including 13 elk farms in Saskatchewan and four in Montana. All this happened in one year! With an approximate escape rate of 1.3 percent, about 2,000 or more potentially infected elk will escape into the wilds in Alberta alone each year once the elk ranching industry is fully established. The possiblities of widespread cataclysmic disease outbreaks in our free-roaming elk herds are imminent, as is genetic pollution and the slow extinction of the elk due to hybridization with farmed red deer.

Because elk and other game ranch wildlife are notorious for escaping from captivity, diseases and genetic pollution are sure to spread to wild populations of elk. Tall game farm fences are broken by falling trees, washed out by flash floods along creeks, buried by snowdrifts that form around the wire, collapsing the fences, or the captive deer walk over the top of the drifted-in fence. Gates on game farm fences are sometimes accidentally left open, and elk wander out. Fences are also sometimes demolished by wild bull elk trying to gain entry to fenced-in areas to mate with captive females. Fences have also been cut by vandals. Moreover, after a few years, game fences corrode, weaken and break, and some species of deer continually test these barriers for opportunities for escape.

All this is not hypothetical, but already stark fact in North America. Unscrupulous dealers have sold elk and red deer hybrids as pure elk, and these have found their way into the wilds. In the particular case I am aware of, it is likely that the hybrids have not withstood wolf predation—at least I hope they have not. Colorado, which allowed red deer ranches for game ranching purposes, is now buying back the red deer and exchanging them for elk. The genetic degradation of our elk, then, is looming with the growth of the deer ranching industry, and has already begun.

The introduction of livestock diseases into our populations of wild elk will increase infection rates in wild as well as domestic ungulates, placing all livestock producers at risk and precluding the hope of making livestock operations free of major diseases.  Much money has been spent on the prevention of livestock infestations in the United States and Canada. The multiple outbreaks of Bovine Tuberculosis on deer ranches in 1990 in western Canada, however, have shown just how fragile such disease-preventive measures can be.

The escape of diseases into wild elk also puts at risk more than the livestock industry. Native people are affected, for the diseases not only destroy populations of one species but can be transmitted to other animal species, putting whole wildlife communities at risk and thereby the welfare and health of subsistence-hunting peoples. Wildlife plagues may also severely damage legitimate sport hunting and a tourist industry that earns much of the $65 billion spent annually on wildlife-related activities on this continent.

Diseases carried by ranched elk would also put the public at risk. Take, for instance, the fatal neurological disease called "scrapie" in sheep, which manifests itself in humans as the dreadful Creutzfeld-Jakob disease, and as "mad cow disease" in British cattle. The disease is transmitted in food via organs of affected livestock, via the growth-promoting pituitary extract derived from slaughtered sheep for injection in people deficient in growth, and via the ingestion of soil contaminated with the infective agent.

The scrapie neurological agent is a virus-like protein that withstands very high temperatures, immersion in formaldehyde or alcohol, protein digesting enzymes, and years of burial in soil; once it enters a new host the disease lies dormant for five or more years. This disease is currently found in ranched elk in the western states.

In sheep, scrapie can be effectively controlled. We eat sheep as lambs, well before the disease organism can saturate the organ systems of the lamb. The disease carrier has not been found in red meat, but only in the neural tissue, bone marrow, lymphatic tissue, the thymus, liver, kidney and spleen. Any infected sheep herd is quickly slaughtered, the carcasses burned, and the raising of sheep prohibited on the infested ground.

In elk we do not even know how scrapie is transmitted, let alone its prevalence in the wilds. The disease cannot be detected in living animals. Free-living elk could get it if they nibbled the bones of sheep that died of scrapie on elk ranges, or they could become infected on game ranches if fed bone or protein meal from infected sheep as a dietary supplement to promote antler growth. Since elk on game ranches are kept to ages not usual in wild populations, for antler production or for reproductive purposes during herd build up, any elk over five years of age sent to slaughter could be a scrapie carrier. Moreover, cutting the carcass with a saw—so neural tissue, cerebrospinal fluid and bone marrow is sprayed over the carcass—transfers the infective agent to the meat.

Scrapie is just one disease. The study of wildlife diseases is a rather new field of science. New diseases are being discovered as old ones appear in surprising new hosts. Granted that elk, unlike domestic stock, have not been kept for thousands of years under unhygienic conditions in close confinement, stressed captive elk are ideal breeding grounds for many diseases. Ranched deer are a veterinarian's dream. Keeping these animals alive means they

A bear's meal, but also the meal of scavengers and soil organisms.
This fertile spot will grow plants for years to come.

THE FUTURE          173

have to be carefully watched and medicated. Granted such treatment with drugs, and granted the possibility of latent scrapie, I personally would not touch a piece of elk meat from a game ranch.

Thus the current thrust by agricultural bureaucracies to make money for game ranchers by ruthlessly pushing for game and hunting ranches presupposes the uncontrollable spread of diseases to wildlife, livestock and people. It also endangers and degrades wildlife via genetic pollution and unleashes the threat of competition by feral populations of ecologically dangerous exotics and hybrids. All this has already happened, though as yet on a moderate scale. It could probably still be rectified, but it would be a hopeless task if widespread game ranching were to become reality.

North America has lived splendidly without this destructive industry that inflicts hideous cruelties on deer, unless you call the sawing off of velvet antlers, without benefit of anesthesia, as happens to Canadian reindeer, anything else. The medicinal value of the organs of elk is uncertain if not nonexistent, and the only effective drugs in velvet antlers may be those injected into some elk before deantlering. Any medical doctor prescribing these drugs for human use would speedily lose his licence for quackery. However, the velvet antlers of the tortured animals are heralded in eastern and southeastern Asia as an aphrodisiac, which raises little more than the hopes of old men but does raise the profits of bordellos from Seoul to Bangkok.

The trophy craze affecting many affluent hunters has already caused much damage too.

Game growers, eager to sell unique trophies, have hybridized elk and other deer. This genetic pollution is the more tragic as large antlers, rather than the result of amateur "genetic engineering," are largely a matter diet and protection. Raising the body and antler size of male ungulates can be accomplished over four or five generations by supplying them a forage with a surplus of digestible protein, energy, and calcium phosphate, and ensuring them undisturbed conditions. Heredity has only a small part to play here. This was proved years ago in the classic experiments of Franz Vogt on European red deer. Of 35 stags he raised to beyond six years of age, 34 exceeded the 100th best stag in antler record book scores, and seven of his stags exceeded the then world record set of antlers.

Our elk are clearly and presently in danger. If they are to remain unadulterated, if we are to pass them on to those who follow, as was done for us, then we need to make sure that elk have large areas of public land to roam and that they are not threatened with poaching and genetic pollution, diseases, and other perils generated by wildlife ranching.

**Boyce, M.S.** and **L.D. Hayden-Wing** (eds.). *North American elk: ecology, behavior and management.* Univ. of Wyoming, Laramie.

This is a technical book with many useful papers by scientists and managers. Also, it's quite inexpensive.

**Egorov, O.V.** 1967. *Wild ungulates of Yakutia.* (Translated from Russian.) U.S. Dept. of the Interior (TT67-51246), Clearing House, Springfield, Va.

This book provides a rare glimpse into the land and wildlife of eastern Siberia. The elk it discusses appears to be a large-bodied representative of the Manchurian wapiti.

**Flerov, K.K.** 1952. *Musk deer and deer.* Fauna of U.S.S.R. Mammals. Vol. No. 2. Acad. Sci. U.S.S.R. Moscow (English trans. U.S. Dept. of Commerce).

This is a classic book on deer, with information on various Asiatic elk.

**Flook, D.R.** 1970. *A study of sex differential in the survival of wapiti.* Canadian Wildlife Service Report, Series No. 11. Queens Printer, Ottawa.

This is a fine technical monograph on elk in the mountain parks of western Canada.

**Geist, V.** and **M. Bayer.** 1988. Sexual dimorphism in the Cervidae and its relation to habitat. J. Zool. London. 214: 45-53.

This is a technical paper which shows how far elk have moved toward cursorial adaptations.

**Heptner, V.G., Nasimovich, A.A.** and **Bannikow, A.G.** 1988. *Mammals of the Soviet Union.* Vol. I, Archtiodactyla and Perissodactyla. Smithsonian Institution. Washington, D.C.

This is a classic, first published in 1961 in Russian and finally available in English translations from the Smithsonian Institution. It gives a fine overview of elk subspecies in Asia.

**Hornocker, M.G.** 1970. *An analysis of mountain lion predation on mule deer and elk in the Idaho primitive area.* Wildlife Monograph No. 21.

This is a fine technical monograph dealing in large part with elk predation.

**Houston, D.B.** 1982. *The northern Yellowstone elk.* Macmillan Publishing Co. New York.

This is a fine technical monograph dealing comprehensively with elk in Yellowstone.

**McCullough, D.R.** 1969. *The tule elk.* Its History, Behavior and Ecology. University of California Press, Berkeley.

A classic. A technical monograph dealing with many aspects of biology and conservation of California elk.

**Murie, O.J.** 1951. *The elk of North America.* Stackpole C. Harrisburg, PA.

Old, but good and still useful is this technical book produced by the Wildlife Management Institute.

**Smith, M.C.T.** 1974. *Biology and management of the wapiti (Cervus elaphus nelsoni) of Fiordland, New Zealand.* New Zealand Deer Stalkers Association, Inc. Wellington, N.Z.

Elk were introduced to New Zealand where they took hold without thriving, as did the red deer. This technical monograph gives some details.

**Thomas, J.W.** and **D.E. Toweill** (eds.). *Elk of North America.* Stackpole Books, Harrisburg, PA.

This is the best current source on elk biology and management. It's a multi-author Wildlife Management Institute monograph that won a Wildlife Society citation. Highly recommended.

**Wemmer, C.** (ed.). *Biology and management of the cervidae.* Proc. Symp. Smithsonian Institution, 1-5 August 1982, Smithsonian Institution Press. Washington, D.C.

Not a book on elk, but on deer with various references to elk. This is a fine technical book, laden with information.